Redneck Spirituality

—Book Two—

Redneck Spirituality

Book One

Book Two

Combined books 1 & 2

Book Three

The Courage of a Butterfly

an autobiographical novel

based on the author's life

Redneck Spirituality

—Book Two—

If Shit's In Your Face Something's Stinkin' In Your Thinkin'

by
E. Egorhh Frank
"Coach Egorhh"

Copyright 2018
by Edmond E. Frank
All rights reserved.
No part of this book may be reproduced
by any means or in any form without
the express permission of the author.

ISBN 978-1-7327328-5-8

Dedication

To my big brother Mark who never saw how the pain

of a seven year old being thrown away,

was what ran his insanely dangerous life—

right up until the gunfight that ended it.

You had nothing to prove to me,

and the truth was, there was no one left,

but you and me.

I loved you then—

I love you now—

But I could not save you.

Only you could slay

the dragons of your mind.

Epigraph

Governments attempt to control

by force of arms—

societies and religions,

by force of mind.

You may not be aware,

but both forces are actively

controlling you right now.

What it takes to be free

IS TRUTH.

Cliché though it might be:

the truth will set you free.

This book is about that truth.

Coach Egorhh

Acknowledgments

To the Sin City writers meet-up group for all their great critiques. And to Bobby Daniels Graphics, who did the excellent work on the cover.

Thanks go to Dee Ann Leger for her excellent editing.

It was great to have such supportive people behind my efforts in putting out this work. Couldn't have done it without cha . . .

Thank you, thank you!

Egorhh

Table of Contents
Redneck Spirituality—Book Two

Part 1—*Life's Laws*
1	About the Laws
3	The Laws of Life (listed)
9	The Bottom Line
13	To Set You Up To Win
15	Some Things You Need To Know
17	This Is A Workbook

Part 2—*Reflections of Life*
21	The Wonderment
22	Peeling Onions
24	My Shit Don't Stink
26	About Pink Paint
28	Omissions
30	Admissions Price
31	The Need to be Accepted
32	Acceptance
33	Adoption
34	On the Law of Present Living
36	Feces
37	Squeezing Oranges
38	Roots
40	Social Creatures
41	No Secrets
42	The Two Sided Mirror
44	A Gifted Few
45	About Respect and Disrespect
46	The Currency of Esteem
47	Vet to Vet
48	Support
49	Waiting on a Friend
50	Validations
51	The Sting of Truth

52	Pretense
53	Expensive People
54	No Fear
55	You Are The Teacher
56	Forgiveness—The Stupid Shit
58	Then There Is FORGIVENESS—The Serious Shit
61	Little Flying Lizards
62	Tigers
63	Feeding Frenzy
64	One's Way of Life
65	About Song
66	Courage
67	Earning Respect
68	Needs and Wants
70	My Viewpoint—In Redneck Speak
73	About Offensive People

Part 3—*Reflections of Love*

77	Unconditional Love
78	Accepting
80	About Relationships
81	Odd Thoughts
82	The Truth About Commitment
95	About Proving One's Love
86	Magnets
88	The truth About Love
90	The Journey of the Heart
92	Living to Our Joy
94	I'm Okay
95	The Other Half of Loving Is Accepting
96	Love and Acceptance
97	Driving a Relationship
98	Control Is Never Love
99	Giving
100	No freedom—No Love
101	The Way You Want It
103	Ultimatums
105	The Relationship Game

- 107   Giving and Accepting
- 108   Diamonds
- 109   Relationships—Needs & Soul Mates
- 111   Soul Mates
- 113   Lovegasm
- 114   Work at a Relationship
- 115   A Single Man's Prayer
- 116   Fearful Needs
- 117   In the End
- 118   Perfect Love
- 119   The Flashbulb of Love
- 120   Sex Is A Beautiful Thing
- 123   In the Energy
- 125   Saying It With Love
- 126   F.U.C.K.
- 127   Grit Your Teeth and Buck-up—

Part 4—*About Politics and Spiritual Law*

- 133   The Collective Consciousness
- 135   Which Side of the Fence
- 136   Left Turn—Right Turn
- 139   Liberals & Conservatives & Spiritual Law
- 141   Repeating History

Part 5—*Reflections of Organized Religion, Spirituality, and a Higher Power*

- 147   The Ocean of God
- 148   The Truth of Our Being
- 149   Putting the Shame on Sex
- 151   Good and Evil?
- 153   It's All Good
- 155   Free Thinkers
- 157   Shepherds and Sheep
- 158   The Ego's Expectations
- 159   Resurrections
- 160   Designated Creator
- 161   Everything We Need

162	Soul Experience
163	In Our Hearts
165	Enlightenment and the Spiritual Warrior
167	Shining Moments
168	Participation
170	Religion
171	Chicken Exits
173	Your Conscious Choice
175	About Beliefs
176	You Are the Winner
179	Now On to the Next Lottery
181	The Choice
183	The Taste-buds of God
188	One and The Same
189	Epilogue

The Assessment
About the Author

Introduction

If you want this book to tell a story and entertain you—it doesn't and it won't. If that is all you feel you want, read a book called "Peter Pan." It's a wonderful fairy tale—not so, this book.

This book is no fantasy. It is about transforming your life—about making it more functional and peaceful. However, there are many who would have no life if they weren't kicking up a little drama to provide excitement. If this is you, then this may ***not*** be the book for you—unless you would like to replace all that drama with some healthy excitement.

As the author, I need to explain that I've always lived life as a redneck. As stated on the cover of Book One, what that means to me is that my life has always been lived on the cusp of crudity. As such, "Redneck" is the language—the crudity—with which I am most comfortable speaking. However, outside of a little crudity I will endeavor to limit myself to good, clear English in the following reflections. After all, they are the reflections of what it means to live life under the Spiritual Laws. I would be negligent if I did not do my best to aid you in understanding them. And please understand also, that some things I feel are best spoken in Redneck.

If you are one who *doesn't* like crudity, and *will* take offense with it—well, feel free to do that ***now***. Don't get your hemorrhoids all in a pucker by reading this book.

While it is not my intention to offend anyone, there are those who never miss an opportunity to take offense. I didn't write this book for them, rather for you who will cherish and appreciate what this book adds to your life—you, the open-minded ones.

The Spiritual Laws are the Laws of Truth—and I have the utmost respect for the truth. That is because like nearly everyone alive, I too was taught the lies. Yet few ever see them until the dysfunctional results have reduced their life to ashes. That is the place from which—like a Phoenix—one then needs to rise, a place where some start looking for the truth. Not so for me. For me it was The Grim Reaper—The Angel of Death—or rather, his presence that sent me searching.

You see, I injured my leg and had a massive pulmonary embolism—a blood clot—in my lungs. I was not expected to live.

In the presence of death, how could I continue with my life's lies? I saw clearly how my whole life was one of pretending to be who others wanted.

At first, the "good Mormon son" my parents wanted, and later, the "limp-dick controllable husband" my wife wanted.

Yes, I pretended so long, that I forgot who I was—but knew, I was someone I didn't like or respect. How could I accept death when it was so clear that I'd never lived a life I could honestly call my own?

And so it was that the angel took pity—gave me a reprieve—the time needed to search out the truth about life, and about me. That was 25 years ago.

THAT TRUTH is what this book is about.

Will it be the same for you? Will you see your own life's lies when The Angel comes for you? Maybe you'll double-down insisting that your life has no lies—not a good bet.

My bet is that you will you want to know the truth. You KNOW that at some unknown time, The Angel WILL come. And you gotta know—he gives very few reprieves.

You might consider this book series to be your own reprieve—
passed from the Angel, through me, to you.

PART ONE

Life's Laws

The Truths of Life

➤

NOTE:

You will likely want to refer back to this section occasionally. Consider placing a page marker on this page for easy referencing. Markers can be purchased at any stationary store—or just fold a piece of tape at the edge to make your own.

About the Laws

The following truths governing life are what some would rather call "Spiritual Laws." I prefer the term Laws of Life. For many, "spiritual," is another way of saying "religious." And this book is not about religion—certainly not "organized" religion. But it does include the concept of a Higher Power—a concept that does not require religion.

A note here for those who, like myself, are likely to get their sphincter all bound up over the linguistics of calling these "Laws." Feel free to call them "Principles" or "Truisms"—or any other word you choose. It is not I who calls them laws, it is life that calls them so. Like gravity, they "just are." If you don't observe the Law of Gravity, it is your body that gets the broken bones. Don't observe these Laws of Truth and your life gets the broken bones—they are the "dysfunctions" upon which you hobble through life.

In Books One and Two the focus is on truth. As mentioned, we have all been taught a boatload of lies with which we are expected to run our lives. This book does not specifically divulged what those lies are. By telling you the following truths, I expect you will be able to see them. Living by those lies always guarantees dysfunction in your life. To change any of it, requires the truth.

We are all built to be right. Being right is the glue that holds our lives together (more on that later). For now, let's just say that there are those who don't have the ability within

the paradigm of their thinking to see—much less move past the lies. For them to understand about these concepts, a Book Three may be a necessity. Problem is, I am not into stroking anyone's resistance. Besides, how does one write a positive book dealing with negativity? And, some say that is exactly what Books One and Two do—you decide.

It is entirely up to you if you want to believe what is offered in this book. It is just that with so many folks hobbling around on their dysfunctions, they are going stagger into you in your life. Do you want

to put up with their shit? Accept these truths, and you will see it coming before it has slimed you.

It has been said that nothing is all black and white—that there are no absolutes. They are not talking about the truth. The truth is always an absolute. The laws are the truth. Base your life on these truths and it will ALWAYS be functional. But base it on those lies. . . .

These laws have always been around. And you may well have come across them written by others using other words. Likely you too, never understood their depth of meaning. *That* only shows up by living them—which few do. *That* is what this book is meant to do—to illustrate them in action. *That,* is my gift to you. Something I received, at the cost of everything I once held dear, but now offer you without expectations. Accept this gift —or not. Again, it is up to you.

In receiving it, will you too pay a price? Yes, likely so. And from experience I guarantee, whatever the price, *it will be worth it.* (More on that later).

A bit melodramatic? Maybe. Still, no matter where you are in the order of all this, that you have this book in your hands says your soul believes there is something here for you. For it is your soul that in every moment of life, is providing the lessons you need.

This is your life, and you are its sole creator . . .

A deep water river often provides a smooth surface. No matter how clear the water may be, given it is deep, likely you will not see to the bottom. If the following laws do not seem all that interesting, it's okay. The reflections of the laws following in the rest of this book should provide you with what you need to see. Looking at life through the truth in these laws provides a very different view—a view you have likely never seen. Seeing what is beneath the surface here, hopefully will intrigue you.

To aid you in understanding, the applicable laws are listed with each reflection.

The Laws of Life

#1—*I am the Creator.*

Most only take this to mean I create my own life. That is true. But to own it requires me to understand that there is nothing in my life that I have not had the deciding factor in creating. It is true, too, that all other Spiritual Laws presented here, are just aspects of this one. As you read through and comprehend the concepts in this book, you will get a sense of how this Law touches upon the infinite.

#2—*Thoughts create.*

Look around you. Everything our species ever created began as a thought in someone's mind. As for the rest, there is an order to the universe. One that speaks to sentience—to feeling, sensing, understanding, creating—like us, but much more. It is a "Higher Power" infinitely beyond what our religions can conceive.

#3—*Thoughts are energy.*

In being our own Creator, we choose in every second of life, the energy with which we are creating. It can only be one of two energies—the energy of **all that is love**, or the energy of **all** that is not love (fear).

#4—*The energy out, returns in kind.*

The energy of your every thought determines what comes to you in life—*love* or *fear*. This is that freedom of choice which is our greatest gift of all Creation. It is this choice which creates the path of our lives and the quality with which we walk.

#5—*The Universe always balances.*

With every sorrowful thing, there is the potential for an equal joy, yet we are the creators in our lives. There is equal joy to be found in every sorrowful event, *If* we will look for, *and* accept it. The truth is, it is we who have chosen the sorrow, and it is we who must seek and choose the joy. The potential for both exists in balance within the universe, and we are but a shift of mind away, requiring no more struggle than the acceptance of our next breath.

#6—*The energy of thoughts must flow.*

Once taken in, the energy of fear stays and is the initial cause of all sickness *if* it is not felt, acknowledged, and then released. Even love energy must be released—given back out—in order to flow.

#7—*Along with being the creator comes responsibility—one cannot BE the Creator and play the blame game.*

One cannot *not* create. Each person must accept responsibility for the totality of creating their life, especially for all thoughts and feeling associated in that process. **Blame is the abdication of responsibility, the greatest of all Mankind's dysfunctional lies.**

#8—*The world is not "out there"—it is "in here."*

It is comprised of every thought, every belief, and every feeling you have. Your world is totally your responsibility because you are the only one who has the ability to respond—the ability to make it better or worse—loving or fearful. **Only you can change your mind.**

#9—*Others are but a mirror for us to see ourselves.*

What we don't like in others is but the reflection of what we don't like in ourselves. If it were not also within us, we could never see it in them.

#10—*The purpose of life is for those lessons.*

When we refuse the learning, the lessons will be presented again, more forcefully until we learn them—or die.

#11—*Self-esteem requires integrity—it is the respect of your soul.*

What our heart feels, what we think, say, and do—all must align as the same, and be coupled with the strength of intension to be in integrity. Integrity commands esteem. Esteem is a far notch above self-respect.

#12—*Our lives are run primarily by our needs—then by our wants.*

As such, our lives are mostly run from an unconscious level. We all know what it is we want—few know what we need to have it. Needs are about the necessities—wants are about the quality.

#13—*Our life is our sole possession—and so it is for everyone.*

We, being the Creator, have all the say in creating our own life—no say in the creation of anyone else's. They are always free to be, say, or do whatever they want—without actual harm to others.

#14—*Change is the constant of the universe.*

Change is fearful. With everything we find fearful, change—the unknown—will be at its core. Fear? Fear is not a constant. It is A choice (Law #3). Sometimes, it is a barometer for change.

#15—*To create a functional life requires one to do one's own thinking.*

The beliefs passed down through the generations, as well as by our religions, are generally accepted as truth. Even when those "truths" serve us falsely, few have the courage to think for themselves. It takes great courage to think differently in the face of family and/or religion. Dysfunction will always come when living the lies passed down to you by others.

#16—*Controlling anything outside ourselves is a fallacy.*

We can only control another in as much as they will let us—or rather, pretend to let us. And our world? See Law 8. Yes, we control our own world, because it lies within us.

#17—*The energy to which we hold fast is what runs our life.*

Mostly it happens from an unconscious level. This is why on the conscious level, forgiveness is so important to our souls. Forgiveness means, to let go of that energy.

#18—Soul to soul pacts are made in the pre-existence.

Each agrees to provide the lessons in life the other needs for the growth of their soul. Those people in your life who it seemed were

especially mean—maybe you asked them to be. Was there a lesson from them that required them to be so?

#19—We are quintessentially, beings of energy.

Our energy affects that of the others around us. We cannot avoid it and are always attracted to those of like energy.

#20—God the Creator—that Higher Power—infuses the energy of the entire universe.

We are part of that energy—we each, are a part and piece of God.

#21—Real love, once given, cannot be taken back.

There are all kinds of interactions that are generally billed as "love"—lust, caring, companionship, even ownership. All that mislabeling notwithstanding, "real love" is an all-or-nothing gift, given without exceptions, expectations, or demands for anything in return. Real love begins with loving yourself. The love you hold within you—for you—*is* the love you give to another.

#22—*We can only feel our own feelings on a conscious level.*

Your love for another is a gift you give to you. As for the feelings, the energy, of others—that is felt at a higher, unconscious part of our minds. Our Soul comprises the total energy of our being—most of which is beyond the conscious. On this conscious level, you can only feel yourself loving them.

#23—*All life happens right now—now is the only time there is for the living.*

The past is dead, and the future belongs to our dreams. We have only **"the now!"**

#24—*Whatever our thoughts dwell upon with energy, is what we are attracting—right now.*

It may be your fondest dream—or your worst nightmare. Some call this "The Law of Attraction." It is simply how we use our energy, in the creation of our lives.

#25—*Your every word is an order to your soul.*

Thoughts create, and if you don't want them manifested into your life, then that thought, and especially every thought once spoken, must be consciously cancelled, **with passion.**

#26—*Change requires truth*.

One cannot change anything about one's thinking unless it is the truth about what one's heart wants. And one cannot change anything about one's life without first changing one's thinking. Change your mind—change your life. Pretending to accept someone else's thinking is to live a pretend life—never sustainable, always dysfunctional.

The Bottom Line

(Much of the following is repeated from Book One)

Y'know, it's hard to be a fresh voice writing about Spiritual Laws and concepts that have been around all down through the ages. Even the ancient greek philosopher, Socrates, talked about them.

"The unexamined life is not worth living."—**Socrates**

Examining and understanding who you are, and what your true responsibilities are in life, is the crux of these Laws of Life. While there are other Spiritual Laws that touch on other matters, the ones listed in this book series, all concentrate on your responsibilities in life.

Fresh? Different? What does this book series have to offer that all those before it didn't? Perhaps it is the fact that in the past, there have been few writers with the cajones to say it like it is. It would be so much easier, and more profitable, to give you a feelie-good workbook.

This is NOT a feelie-good workbook!

For many, were it to be written in terms that make it feel good, it would only validate their existing dysfunctional thinking, and change nothing. The things you need look at, that can and do change your life, are those things that DON'T feel good. The truth of these Spiritual Laws does not depend upon your acceptance. If you are living a lie, seeing the truth will always be uncomfortable because it demands change—change never feels good until after it has become familiar. So decide now if you want it. Living a dysfunctional life may not be all that enjoyable, but it does feel safer than making changes. So now, lets talk about the lies.

It is not "politically correct" to tell you just how badly your life has been "anal-lyzed." Shit! Those dysfunctional lies you have been taught upon which you "should" base your life—it might help to know that "should," is merely the shit from between someone else's ears.

But hey, that is just the human condition. A smell is just a smell—we are the ones who say when shit stinks. Face it: no one finds the smell of their own shit all that repulsive—well, do you? If you did, it would make it difficult to live with yourself—wouldn't it? It is only other people's shit we think stinks—no matter out of which end it comes.

Politics be damned! It also begs acknowledging—clearly—just who those liars are that wiped all that "should" off onto your life. They are your **parents,** your **religions**—*all those whom you love and respect*. Why else would you just accept those lies without question? Just know, it was never a deliberate thing. They accepted it all before you, same as you. Consider: what if the person telling you all that "should," had been someone you didn't even know—some redneck, maybe like me?

Yes, puts it all in a different light—doesn't it? I encourage you to think for yourself, and to question every word you read in these pages, and everything you are told from now on—forever! This is what it takes to be free—for your thoughts to be truly your own.

And the "shoulds" that lie between your own ears—are they indeed, your own? Do they uplift and nourish you with truth? The thing about shit is that it is about what has nourished you. What makes it stink so badly, is when it has never nourished you, likely because it came from between someone else's ears. Instead of nourishing, it has made you a stinking victim in life.

To be honest, didn't I just tell you how *your life has been* "anal-lyzed"—how you have been a "stinking victim?"

> *Whoa, hey! Have I also been "shoulding" on you?—*
> *or am I offering you a choice?*

The key words here are, *"your life has been."*—**PAST TENSE!**

Point is; that was the truth about your past. It is now up to you if that will be the truth in your future. Within the cocoon of these Spiritual Laws, that victimized pupa from your past, now has a chance to become a butterfly.

And me?—What do I get for rubbing all this truth in your face? I fully expect *some* will want to crucify me. Hell, Socrates was put to death for this same act of politically incorrect social disobedience. My purpose in exposing you to these truths is simply to offer you an opportunity to make your world—and mine—a little better place. I have no desire to be a Preacher—or Guru. I'm just tired of seeing this shit-storm of dysfunction swirling all around—and knowing the reasons behind it all—and yet not caring enough to open my mouth and risk condemnation. Twenty-five years ago the Angel gave me a reprieve. This book series just may be his reason.

This is not a big book, but if you're paying attention, it will be a long read—Take your time.

It is meant to be a workbook. Whether it is a hard copy or digital—doesn't matter. To work it, you will need a notebook, preferably one that is a binder. At some point you may need more space and want to add a page here or there. In the beginning, write only on the right side page. The reason for this will be explained later. Write down the title and page number of the reflection, then answer the questions and do the exercises.

How much this book will add to your life will be determined by how much work you are willing to put into it. Some will buy this book and read it for the information. They want knowledge—they don't want change. That is okay. For those who do want change, the writing is the easy part. I guarantee that if you work it, your life will be different—better.

And, just maybe you will want to make a difference for someone else—perhaps even one of those liars whom you love. Without you, they likely will never have a clue about those lies. Pass this book on, or better yet, buy another and pass that one on. The debt everyone owes to that Higher Power for the privilege of being alive *is to live a life that makes a difference.*

Could be that—like me—*now's your chance . . .*

To Set You Up To Win

As explained, *Book One* has sixteen of the Laws listed. This book has expanded that to twenty-six, and includes aspects of *love and love-relationships,* as well as the really dangerous shit to consider: *organized religions, God, spirituality, and*—oh my God—*politics (always cheesy shit).*

Just remember: I am not telling you what to think. You decide that. But it is a moot point if you decide *not* to think. If that is your choice, then it is pretty-much a given that the energy you are deciding with is *not* loving. You see, I am merely asking you to consider *how* you think—what is the energy in which you think? If you accept the truth in Law 4, it states the there are only two energies: love or fear. This book is written in the energy of *love.* When reading it, I ask you to think for yourself, but that you think in the energy of *love*, not *fear.*

All "organized religions" work through the energy of fear. The fear of what that Higher Power they claim as their authority—God—Allah—Hari Krishna—etc—might do if you disobey. And the fear that your connection with that Higher Power rests solely with them. You get the point?

Yes, I told you this is NOT a feelie-good workbook!

Then, there is love and loving relationships—love is where a lot of thinking really gets to stinking—and where a lot of folks get out the pink paint. What those involved may think is love, those not involved can see it for what it is—not love, but fear

So, if in the process of reading this book, your cheese starts sliding off of your cracker—let it. You may find you then have an opportunity to take a breath of fresh air. Your cheese has been moldering and fermenting in all that fear, and you no longer notice the stink. It may be the only way your soul has of showing you how badly your cheese stinks.

Your soul is the part of that Higher Power charged with showing you, the things you need to see—or rather, the lessons you need to learn in this life. No doubt there will be some things in this book that won't feel good. Is it possible that pointing those things out, is why your soul put it in your hands in the first place?

Some Things You Need To Know

(Reprinted From Book One)

You have read the Laws—pretty benign, don't you think? Now it's time to look at what they mean in life. This is where things may start not-feeling-so-good. ***This*** is where you will start seeing your viewpoint of life may not be the truth. ***This*** is where you will start seeing the lies you have been ***taught to believe.***

Some of the following reflections will merely feel "off," and you will probably see it as negativity—blame it on me, the writer. ***Some*** will tweak your sense of propriety. ***Some*** you may feel are outrageously blasphemous—

Good!

As all speak of your own perceptions, these are the things that you need look at—the things that would mean change in your life—were you to accept them. The simple fact is, your soul sees the truth in them, but your conscious mind sees only the change they would require in you, ***and is afraid.***

You now have only one of two ways to go:

Gather your courage and change—or accept whatever dysfunctions you may have going in your life that you've been telling yourself you want to change, ***and give-up right here.***

The real issue you will then have to deal with is the fact that you have already been exposed to the Laws—to the truth of life. If you are not specifically aware of the lies you have been taught to believe, they will soon become apparent—right in your face. Again, your soul will see to it, because it is your soul that brought you to these pages. If any peace, love, or joy is somehow missing in your life—and you truly want it—then gather your courage ***and keep on reading.***

Bottom line: I am probably the only person you will ever meet who has the right—even the obligation—to say this last thing to you. This is because

I HAVE BEEN THERE.

When the Angel comes to take you home, he will either pick up a hero or a coward—
that is the choice you have before you—

RIGHT NOW!

This Is A Workbook

You likely will feel a need to know how you did as far as scoring yourself—or not. If that thought in your mind right now is that you aren't interested in your score, then count yourself as failing—failing to be honest with yourself.

Let's face it. This book would not be in your hands—or digitally in your face—if you did not want something from it. Here is what I am asking you to do. Make the following notations near the title of each reflection, whether in your hardcover or notebook.

1. With every reflection presented, if you agree without resistance, just put a check mark. These are things that were in your belief system to begin with.

(✓)

2. If the reflection has pointed out something more something new—then put a check with a plus sign.

(✓ +)

3. If you feel anything negative, or even just an "off" feeling concerning it, then you have some resistance going on—it is a good thing when you think for yourself. Put a circle.

(O)

4. **If you don't understand it—after having re-reading the full applicable Laws listed—that is also considered resistance. Put a circle with a question mark beside it.**

(O?)

5. **If you understand, but don't agree, put an X beside your circle of resistance.**

(OX)

6. **And if it is something you don't agree with to the extent that you resent it, put an exclamation mark next to that X.**

(OX!)

7. **If at anytime you find yourself in agreement with any showing a circle of resistance, simply add a check mark.**

O✓—O?✓—OX✓—OX!✓

NOTE:
Please understand, these are reflections of the Laws of Truth. You may notice some may be very similar, just presented using different scenarios. That's right, they have been repeated. Inside one of them is an explanation for this. **Watch for it.**

At the end of this book, you will find another explanation, on how to assess your progress through this book. **Do NOT cheat yourself by flipping forward to read it before you have finished doing the work.**

PART TWO

Reflections of Life

In the Light of the Laws

The Wonderment

Until you've looked inside yourself,
you'll never know the wonderment,
of knowing just what you can do,
of seeing who you really are.
The depths of your courage . . .
The breadth of your heart . . .
The heights to which
your soul can soar . . .
With so much magnificence to discover,
why would you not want to find?
When only stopping you are your fears . . .
the imaginary dragons of your mind.

Peeling Onions

This book is about peeling an onion—the onion of your beliefs. In looking at the way you think about everything you will find that *who* you are, is *what* you believe. Unfortunately, what you believe is often based on a whole lot of lies. This book is about looking at some of those lies and replacing them with truth. Indeed, you will find it is like peeling an onion: There will always be another layer to peel underneath—and often, there will be tears.

In general, the lies come from your society—other people wanting you to live your life to suit theirs, wanting to control you, and essentially enslave you. You have been taught to see yourself as a victim with other people holding the reins, the power in your life—your government, your religion, your parents, your significant others, etc.

In changing any of that, the first step is getting a clear understanding that you are the creator of your life and that only you, hold the responsibility—the ability-to-respond—to everything in it. That is Law number one—"I am the creator." Beginning with this law, you will start to see the truth of it all. And you will begin to peel the onion.

These spiritual laws I have offered you in this book are the truths. Peeling your onion and replacing the lies will be a

journey—a wonderful journey you won't regret taking, regardless of the tears. And these truths are only the beginning. You will learn about many more—and will apply the nuances of them all in your life. There is great joy in living the truth and being the master of your own life.

The responsibility of holding the reins of your life is a scary thing and requires more courage than most people have. Just remember to (1) *live your life in love and not fear*—you then (2) *need no courage*, because courage requires you to first have fear. (3) *One cannot love in the space of fear*—it is one of the laws. (4) *There can be no fear if you are loving.*

 I've said it four times. I hope you have taken at least one to heart. *Living in love is what brings joy to life*—there, that's five. *Five is enough, don't you think?*

———— — — — ————

See Life's Laws:
1   I am the creator.
2   Thoughts Create.
3   Thoughts are energy: Loving, or not loving (fear).
8   The world is not "out there"—it is "in here."
15   One must do one's own thinking.

Questions and/or exercises to consider:
- **This jour**ney is sometimes called "The Hero's Journey." What do you think? *Write about it.*
- **Are you** seeing some of those lies yet? Do you feel the burn? *Again, write about it.*
- **Might you** actually be enslaved by the lies? Do you want to be free—or do you think this is all a little bit "out there?" *Yup, write about it.*
- **Can you** afford the price of not looking at it—of not examining the lies you've accepted, and by which you've been living your life?

My Shit Don't Stink

As mentioned in the beginning section of this book (in The Bottom Line), let's talk about shit—or rather the stink of it. Have you ever noticed how when two dogs meet, the first thing they do is stick their nose into the other dogs ass. The reason is simple: They don't have sweat glands in their skin, and so they smell each others ass in order to be able to recognize one another's scent. They don't judge if the other's butt smells good or bad—a smell is just a smell. Any judgment they do, has already been done. By reading the other's demeanor they already know if that other dog is loving or unloving—a danger, or not a danger—and have decided to get acquainted.

We humans are supposed to be the advanced species. Why is it we aren't that smart? Why do we judge everything about one another as good or bad? Why is the smell of our own shit acceptable, while the smell of another's is not? For us, smelling one another's butt is unnecessary. Even so, we too have eyes, and can see. We too only need judge if the other is loving or unloving—a danger, or not a danger—someone we want to know or not.

If you own dogs, you know that you are part of their pack—hopefully their leader. If a dog has any fault there, it would be its loyalty. When faced with unconditional love, we humans seldom respond with love. When we have no love within ourselves, we have none for another. Within our own species, it is seldom we encounter unconditional love. It is the fault of our teachers who confuse us with the idea we must love others, while negating the idea of loving ourselves. How insane is that?

See Life's Laws:
3   Thoughts are energy: Loving, or not loving (fear).
4   The energy out, returns in kind.
8   The world is not "out there"—it is "in here."
1   I am the creator.

Questions and/or exercises to consider:
- **What does** all this tell you? In fact, what's it all about—what is the underlying thought here?
- **Is it about** the stink of shit?
- **Is it about** judging things good or bad?
- **Is it about** the behavior of dogs?
- **Is it about** the energy we choose to live within—loving or not loving?
- **About some** things, our species is down-right fucking stupid. What are those things?
- **You may** come back and answer this last question after completing the rest of this book

About Pink Paint

It's been mentioned how our society demands we paint our humanity with the pink paint of "a gentleman" or "a lady"—that we must wear a facade—because if others could see who we really are, we would not be acceptable.

But making ourselves out to be fakes and frauds is but one of society's dishonest demands. There are many other lies we have been pressed to believe, and on which to base our thinking—indeed, our very lives. Many of those other lies were taught by our parents, our friends, our teachers----and oh yes, especially by our religions.

We have been taught so many lies that our lives have come to revolve around a game—a game called *blame*. Blame and control, instead of love, our relationships now consist of little more than playing that game.

The Reflections offered in these workbooks are about showing you life from the viewpoint of truth—as reflected by the Laws of Life. The first, and most important law being that you are the creator of your life—it designates your responsibility in life—and means basically, that "blame" can no longer be in the vocabulary of yours. Without blame, you need no control over others.

See Life's Laws:
3   Thoughts are energy: Loving, or not loving (fear).
4   The energy out, returns in kind.
8   The world is not "out there"—it is "in here."

Questions and/or exercises to consider:
- **We all** have our own traits that make us human. What are yours?
- **Can anyone** really accept you—indeed, know you—if you hide those traits?
- **Do you** see yourself as a loving individual? Why?
- **How much** of your relationship with your significant is about blame, and the struggle to control? The next time you find yourself in a "lover's spat," ask yourself that question.
- **Surely you** can see how fucked-up the pink paint of a facade really is? —In fact, how fucked-up are all the lies that you have been taught.
- *The main exercise of this book is now, to write down the lies as they become obvious to you. Use the blank left side paper in your notebook/binder and put it next to whatever reflection you are currently writing about.*

Omissions

(Reprinted From Book One)

Just because someone is telling me the truth—just not the full truth—does not excuse them from being a liar anywhere except in their own twisted mind. If I accept another person's lie as my own truth without searching my soul—well, that just makes me lazy, and ignorant.

Regardless of my good intentions, your journey in life is your own. Don't just believe these thoughts of mine without first asking your heart. It is your heart that connects you to your soul. Don't be a lazy ignor-anus by accepting something your heart doesn't feel is true.

I've told you nothing within this book that I don't believe to be true, and no lies of omission unless they be out of the ignorance of my own humanity—I am searching, just like you. The fact you have this book in your hand confirms that about you. Again, my journey has lasted some 25 years. That is a lot of time to be searching one's own soul and one's world for the truth. If your search has just begun, I wish it to be as wondrous as mine has been.

See Life's Laws:
15   One must do one's own thinking.
7   Along with being the creator comes responsibility.
2   Thoughts create.
8   The world is not "out there." It is "in here."
10   The purpose of life is for those lessons.

Questions to consider:
- **Do you** ever tell incomplete truths—leaving out defining parts that would otherwise sway your meaning?
- **Those things** your parents, your religious leaders, and society told you were the truth—did you just accept them as being true? Most everyone in the world does, y'know.
- **Do you** believe the lies now? List every lie you now see you have believed.
- **Your soul** always knows the truth, both the truths about life, and the truths about *your* life. But few are willing to look inside. If you work this workbook, you will look—and you will write down what you see. The only question is: Do you have the courage? Any lies you may find yourself living, will demand you change your thinking—and your life.

This is the full truth of this book—nothing left out.

Admissions Price

Making someone unacceptable is always about playing the game of control. It is about me, demanding you change something about yourself—that being, the price of my acceptance. What I don't see, is that I am only buying your pretense. What *you* don't see, is that whatever the demand—whatever my price—you are being cheated. For my acceptance is also, only a pretense. And the real price we both pay is one of honor. No one plays this game unless they are holding the other responsible for their own choice of feeling—something that is never honorable.

One's honor is always the admissions price for playing the game of control.

See Life's Laws:
13   Our own life is our sole possession. Just so, it is for everyone.
16   We only control ourselves.
11   **Self-esteem requires integrity.**
26   Change requires the truth of one's heart.

Questions and/or Exercises:
- **When the** issue involves something someone is doing that threatens your physical security, do you think you need to make that person's actions unacceptable?
- **What about** that person?
- **What if** they are doing something that you simply don't like?
- Do you think other people must live their lives to suit you?

The Need to be Accepted

Everyone wants to be accepted. It is a basic human need. Some try to fill that need by trying to change themselves to fit in with others. Some try to change others to be a fit for themselves.
For me, it is about being true to who I am, then looking for others who fit into my life, just being who they are.

Trying to change others, to be who I want, never works. My feelings are the only ones within my control—and accepting, only takes me accepting them, and always works. When I stop trying to change them, they feel free to be who they are. Then we both will know if we fit into each other's lives.

It is only when I can accept people for exactly who they are, that I get to know who the other is, and have the people in my life who I want to be there.

See Life's Laws:
13   Our own life is our sole possession. Just so, it is for everyone.
16   We only control ourselves.
26   Change requires the truth of one's heart.

Questions and/or Exercises:
- **Can you** see, that one of the lies Society has taught us, is that we must have a facade that is acceptable to everyone? Describe your own facade.
- **Do you** think that facade serves or hinders us? *How?*

Acceptance

Accepting someone simply means you don't try—nor even have a need—to change them. Accepting them has nothing to do with liking them.

When someone does not accept you, being exactly who you are, it is not necessarily a bad thing. Could it be, it is just your higher self—yours and theirs—saying stay away, we don't belong together? Theirs is simply saying, "I am someone who won't be happy unless I get to change you."

Still, given this understanding, you can accept them even when they won't accept you. Just heed your higher self and move on in life. Find someone else who accepts and likes, you just being you.

See Life's Laws:
4   The energy out, returns in kind.
17   What we hold with energy runs our life.
19   We are quintessentially, beings of energy.
13   Our own life is our sole possession. Just so, it is for everyone.
16   We only control ourselves.

Questions and/or Exercises:
- **When someone** will only accept you if you change yourself to suit them, can they ever really be a friend?
- **What are** your minimum requirements for being friends? *List them.*
- **Are any** of these things "inherently you"—something only you might require?
- **Is genuinely** caring for one another on your list?

Adoption

People adopt for one of only two reasons: Because they want "that child." Or because they want the child they could not have and are accepting "that child" as a surrogate. A surrogate child will never be good enough, nor will it ever be loved. It is not the "real thing." Is it any wonder that the "higher power"—that God— did not give those particular parents a child?

Will that child love such a parent?—Yes, very likely. That is what innocent children often do. But will that parent know it? If one has not the ability to give it, does one have the ability to know when love is given?

As a surrogate myself, I would ask that if you don't want "that child," only for itself, then please—just get a puppy. A puppy will never grow up to know, **it is not good enough.**

See Life's Laws:
21   Real love, once given, cannot be taken back.
8   The world is not "out there"—it is "in here."

Questions and/or Exercises:
- **Are you** considering adoption?
- **Are you** clear as to your reasons?
- **Is it because you want "that" child?**
- **If that** is so, then make a list of everything that you like about "that" child.
- **If your** list is short---reconsider

On the Law of Present Living

We are all just painters, painting on the canvas of our lifetime. A painter who has no concept of its size, yet the living always takes place at the point of their brush, in the place called now.

One paints—creates—from the pallet of one's past. On it are placed all the colors of the rainbow. Yet some painters choose to mix the colors by their fears: muddy browns, dark grays, even blacks. They prefer to paint their lives as the storm, and sometimes—though not often—painting the rainbow, like an unattainable mirage.

For the rainbow is comprised of the pure colors of love, the colors of pure joy—the highest essence of the creator. Other painters use those colors in beautiful summer scenes, with sunlight streaming, flowers, clouds and birds—beauty and joy in every stroke.

What separates the painters and their scenes? They all are creating on the canvases of their lives, yet the pictures are so different. Some might say that the painters of the storms must somehow want the turmoil of their lives.

Yes, it is true that not all painters' hearts are drawn to the pure colors of the rainbow, to the beauty in the purity of love. But the bottom line truth here is simple: some paint with their fear, while the others, with their love.

And what of the canvas? What of the limits of one's lifetime? Is it true that some paint tiny figures, using only little strokes, and in the end the canvas is mostly white, leaving little of themselves to mark this world?

Others paint with wide sweeping strokes of loving abandon, or raging fear—strokes, which in the end fling paint off the canvas; drops of their love, or fear, marking eternity.

——— — — — ———

See Life's Laws:
23   Now is the only time there is.
1   I am the creator.
3   Thoughts are energy: Loving, or not loving (fear).
8   The world is not "out there"—it is "in here."

Questions and/or Exercises:
- **Do you** paint with the colors of your love—or your fear?
- **Is your** painting one of a fearful need to control others—even those you think you love?
- **Hitler, literally** and figuratively, was a painter. He painted the ugliness and stench of the Third Reich. Ironically, some of his earlier painted scenes of beauty were of the places he literally laid to waste, in later life. Is that the kind of picture you would paint with your fear?
- **I too,** have left some shit-stains stinking up my picture. The only way to flush it clean is with the love I paint with now. And so I write these books. What will you do?
- **How will** your picture change between now and when it is finished?
- **Will you** take this book, and make it your reprieve?

Feces

There are many things that obstruct our ability to know and give love. Shame is only one. "Shames" and "shoulds"—such are, as the feces of other people's minds that they would heap upon us. To accept it does not mean we will be fertilized and grow to be better; it just means our viewpoint of life will be obstructed and stink.

See Life's Laws:
3   Thoughts are energy.
8   The world is not "out there"—It is "in here."
15   To create a functional life requires one to do their own thinking.

Questions and/or Exercises:
- **Write down** some of the times you have felt shame.
- **Now note** which were the times that others wiped that shame off onto you, and which were the times, you did the wiping all by yourself.
- **Read Law 3**—Is it possible to love someone when immersed in the feces of fear—yours or theirs?

Squeezing Oranges

When life squeezes you, don't expect orange juice. You get to see what's really inside you. Remember, *you are the creator,* and that's why you arranged to be squeezed. There is something you need to see—in you.

Don't believe you arranged to be squeezed? Look again. You *don't* have the ability to see that one, if you *won't* look at what it is in you, that you need to see.

See Life's Laws:
11   Self-esteem requires integrity.
10   The purpose of life is for those lessons.

Questions and/or Exercises:
- **Do you** agree that everyone occasionally gets squeezed in life?
- **What is** it, that comes out of you?
- **Do you** understand that this is the thing your soul demands you look at in order to grow?
- **You don't** believe it? Then consider: Is denying your soul's orders likely to be a healthy thing?

Roots

We all have roots. Like the plants, we too, need a root system to channel the energy of acceptance, respect, and love needed to nurture us in life. It is the soil of our family heritage that normally supports us. Their acceptance is like the water that flows the nutrients. Their respect propels it all along. And love? Without love, all life within our souls would simply wither.

The ecosystem of our family plot is needed for our growth and survival. Yet we are not exactly plants. For we have the ability to move about. This ability serves us well, when occasionally there is no acceptance to be had, or little nutrition to be found in the rocky ground of ones judgmental family soil.

Oh, some may choose to whither in life, but those with courage will pull their roots, and find more fertile soil, where nutrients flow in the acceptance of others. Perhaps they will no longer have the solace of the family plot, the comforting familiarity of it, but they still have the ability to be nurtured. In fact, they then have the ability to grow far beyond what their family plot ever had to offer.

Should one call this a gift, or a curse? Certainly some will curse them for the very action of moving. "Ungrateful little . . ." Yes, I've heard it too.

And perhaps, it simply doesn't matter—not to one who just accepts "what is." Perhaps one then becomes the nurturing soil those orphaned others need. Perhaps one then starts a new family plot. Perhaps one then leaves a new family legacy. Perhaps then, the whole world is nurtured. Perhaps. . . .

See Life's Laws:
5   For every sorrowful thing, there exists the potential for equal joy. The Universe always balances.
19 We are quintessentially, beings of energy.
12 Our lives are run first by our needs—then our wants.
18 Soul to soul pacts are made in the pre-existence.

Questions and/or Exercises:
- **How well** does your family plot support you in life? *Explain.*
- **If it doesn't**, have you moved on?
- **If it doesn't**, and you haven't, will you?

Social Creatures

We are social creatures. We all need each other. It is the connection itself we need so much to feel. Social creatures don't do life well alone. Yet aren't we all—on that higher, spiritual level of our minds and hearts—connected? When one gets past the pain, that energy of fear, with which we cloud our minds—gets to know the energy of one's love fully—*then* is when one sees that higher spiritual connection, and really feels it. *Then,* is when we need no one—yet, connect with everyone.

See Life's Laws:
3 Thoughts are energy: Loving, or not loving (fear).
17 What we hold with energy runs our life.
19 We are quintessentially, beings of energy.

Questions and/or Exercises:
- **How social** a creature are you?
- **Do you** play the "Lone Ranger," crying inside for that connection, but afraid to reach out for it with love? Write about any long, cold, lonely ride you've taken in your past.
- **Do you know** that if you don't have love for yourself, you have none to offer others?

No Secrets

There are no secrets, just things we refuse to see consciously. In my higher mind, I know everything about you—and you, me. On that level, there are no secrets. And on that level, we are so much more than we can ever consciously conceive.

See Life's Laws:
19   We are quintessentially, beings of energy.
20   We are part of the energy that comprises God.

Exercises Questions and/or:
- **What if** who we are on that level, is simply love?
- **And were** that true, do you think being conscious of—that believing it as fact—might cause us to treat one another better?
- **Will you** consider believing it?

The Two-sided Mirror

There have been known cases in which someone, blind from birth, has been given the ability to see. They literally had to learn what they were seeing by the use of the previous experience of it–touch, smell, hearing. An apple was not recognized until the eyes were closed and it was held, smelled, and then tasted. Just so, I experience you, only through the existing experience of me—kind of like looking in a mirror.

There is a Spiritual Law which states: You are but a mirror in which I can see me. Basically, it says that what I see in you that I don't like, is but a reflection of what I don't like in me. Kind of like looking at each other through a two-sided mirror; we each see only aspects of ourselves.

Isn't it scary that the person we each see when regarding one another, is always a perfectly shielded reflection of our self. Isn't it amazing that we communicate at all? Do you see how when looking at our reflection, there is always a choice: To war with everything unlovable in ourselves, or to love everything in our own perfect grace? It's all there to see—and it's all about me when looking through a two-sided mirror at you.

The real question is; to see through that two-sided mirror, am I willing to see the true beauty of you, knowing I must use eyes I have never used? Will I look inward, close my eyes and smell, and taste, and savor? Will I own the

exquisite essence of my aroma, taste the delicious flavors of me? Will I choose to experience, and be nourished, by the truth of all this beauty within me? And then—only then, reach out with that energy to experience you, and what you have to add to me. The energy of pure love is required to see through a two-sided mirror. Were it to be given a name, I believe that two-sided mirror could be called "Namaste'"

Note: *'Namaste' is a cultural and religious word from the Hindu religion that roughly translated means: My Divine soul recognizes the Divine soul in you.*

See Life's Laws:
3   Thoughts are energy: Loving, or not loving (fear).
7   Blame is the abdication of responsibility.
9   Others are but a mirror for us to see ourselves.
8   The world is not "out there"—it is "in here."
19   We are quintessentially, beings of energy.
15   One must do one's own thinking.

Questions and/or Exercises:
- **Do you** find it easier to look for and see the darkness, the negative, the fearful part of yourself?
- **Do you** realize that this is as it is, for nearly everyone?
- **Wouldn't it** be so much better to look for and find the love?
- **If you did**, how would your life be different.

A Gifted Few

It's all about the lessons . . .

Mostly we ignore them. Some take them to the grave, unacknowledged, unlearned—and un-lived. Sometimes it takes the final whispers from Death himself, to speak of them in a way we will hear. Only a courageous few then receive the gift of Death's lessons, and survive long enough to live them.

See Life's Laws:
10   The purpose of life is for those lessons.
18   Soul to soul pacts are made in the pre-existence.

Questions and/or Exercises:
- **Do you** think that Death's lessons are the gift this book is offering you? This is what I intend it to be—a gift.
- **Do you** understand that within this gift—this reprieve—this book, there are no expectations being held by me that you accept it? Some will—some won't; what is your choice and why?
- **This gift** was given me, and not offering it to you would be unthinkable?
- **If it helps** make your life better, will you do any less than offer it to someone you love?

About Respect and Disrespect

Respect is something I think and feel—and yes, do—toward someone. Respect uplifts us both. It is uplifting in spirit, as well as in standing in the community.

Disrespect now, is not such a mutual thing. Yes, I think it and feel it. And most of all, disrespect is something I do. Thing is—given someone who has self-respect—it doesn't necessarily bring down that person's energy. Nor does it lower that person's standing in the community.

But it will always have those effects upon me.

See Life's Laws:
19   We are quintessentially, beings of energy.

Questions and/or Exercises:
- ➤ **On that** soul level we are all spirits of equal magnificence. Don't you think that requires a certain respect, no matter who they are being here and now?
- ➤ **Sometimes that** is a hard feat to do honestly. If you are unwilling to do it, will you at least respect your soul by not disrespecting them?

The Currency of Esteem

Respect is the currency of a person's esteem. A generous person gives it freely and abundantly upon first meeting another. Then, depending upon that new person's integrity, more might be given, or all might be lost.

But sometimes, as in one Vet to another, there is a debt that is beyond the currency of simple respect. Can it be any other way, when a person has been willing to put their life on the line with yours?

See Life's Laws:
11   Self-esteem requires integrity.
13   Our own life is our sole possession. Just so, it is for everyone.
19   We are quintessentially, beings of energy.

Questions and/or Exercises:
- **If you** are not a Vet, can you understand?
- **If you** are, do you need an explanation?

Vet to Vet

Some fought—Some died . . .

Hell, just being a vet

says you put your life

on the line . . .

with mine.

What our differences now

may not reflect,

is the fact that you,

just being a vet,

will always command

this vet's respect!

Support

Some say that having my own cheering section is necessary to a joyful life. It's true—but only when I am among the supporting members.

See Life's Laws:
19   We are quintessentially, beings of energy.
6   The energy of thoughts must flow.

Questions and/or Exercises:
- **Does your** world revolve for you, or with you?
- **Do you** give as much as you take?
- **Do you** find joy in serving others? *Again, discuss.*

Waiting on a Friend

All we really get coming into this life, is a little time. It could be said that time is life.

So when someone repeatedly makes appointments with me, then asks me to wait . . .

What they are saying to me is: ". . . my time is more important than yours: my life, worth more than yours."

To wait patiently for them to get ready is to allow myself to fall victim. Likely, it is not a conscious thing in their mind. And it is to definitely validate this viewpoint they are expressing of me, into my own mind. Is giving my time—my life—away to a friend really such an admirable thing? In accepting the situation, are we either one, being a friend?

Truth is, if you don't respect my time: you don't respect me—and in time, by allowing it, neither will I.

――――― ― ― ― ―――――

See Life's Laws:
13   Our own life is our sole possession. Just so, it is for everyone.
10   The purpose of life is for those lessons.
18   Soul to soul pacts are made in the pre-existence.

Questions and/or Exercises:
- Do you often make your friends wait?
- **If so** and they refused to wait, would you still consider them your friend?
- **Is it possible** that it is you not being a friend? ***Discuss it with them.***

Validations

Whenever the shit's in your face, it's either a lesson, a test, or a validation. Lessons and tests are usually given by a teacher. Does this mean that validations are to tell you that you got the lessons, have passed the tests and are now teachers?

Not really! Truth is, you—that is, your soul—was always your teacher. Others and events, are just the lessons your soul prepared. Yes, when not learned and passed, the lessons and tests just get harder. But when passed—

The validations? —The validations get absolutely orgasmic!

See Life's Laws:
18   Soul to soul pacts are made in the pre-existence.
10   The purpose of life is for those lessons.

Questions and/or Exercises:
- **Everyone has** some reoccurring shit that keeps splattering them in the face. What's yours?
- **What do you** think the lesson behind it could be?
- **If you find** it easy to answer this last question—that is *not* it. Whatever the true lesson, it is one you do *not* want to look at. **Question is, will you?**

The Sting of Truth

People will always talk. But when we get angry with what they say about us, perhaps it would be wise to remember; the angrier we are, the more their words have carried the sting of truth.

See Life's Laws:
9   Others are but a mirror for us to see ourselves.

Questions and/or Exercises:
- ➤ **Has someone said** something about you recently that really pissed you off? ***Write it down.***
- ➤ **Now what** part of it do you know is true?
- ➤ **Is there** a part that you don't believe is true?
- ➤ **Are you** willing to look with honesty? The part you know to be true, is not the part that pisses you off—take a look at the other part. There is something there you don't want to see.

Pretense

Change? —Change most often comes on the heels of discomfort or necessity, but only when the change is about you. As for changing others, the game of control is just too strong. It has always gotten you what you wanted of others—*or so you believe*. But you don't see that the game is really one of pretense. Any change you may demand and get from others, is merely a pretense.

Real change is always personal—something no one can do to, or for you. Change is something one cannot do, except for one's self.

See Life's Laws:

16   We only control ourselves.
13   Our own life is our sole possession. Just so, it is for everyone.
26   **Change requires** the truth of one's heart.
8   **The world** is not "out there"—it is "in here."
24   **What we** dwell upon with energy—is what we attract.

Questions and/or Exercises:
- **Are you** aware that changing your mind can be an instantaneous thing?
- **Do you** know that the resulting change in your life can also be instantaneous?
- **Don't think** so? You're right!—But only because your world will always come to you the way you see it. *Y'know?*

Expensive People

Expensive people like to take offense. It's not that I ever intended to give offense—fact is—it is not that I did.

Offense is not something one can *"give,"* rather something one must *"take."* With the taking, one demands payment of your energy. Ah, the expense of having people like that in your life . .

Maybe expensive people are simply not worth having around. They just take your energy—while giving nothing back. With expensive people, it is not who you are, but who they want you to be. And more often than not, the "who" you are, is only a figment of their own imagination.

It's not that I'm stingy or poor. What they have is just not something I'm buying. I'm choosy about how I spend my energy in this life.

See Life's Laws:
8   The world is not "out there"—it is "in here."
19   We are quintessentially, beings of energy.
13   Our own life is our sole possession. Just so, it is for everyone.

Questions and/or Exercises:
- **Do you** need to be more choosy about how and with whom you spend your life?
- **Who in** your life is expensive?
- **Being as** this is your one and only life, does anyone have the right to make demands on how you spend it?
- **Do you** ever make such demands upon others? Are you an expensive person?

No Fear

A man is not brave who has no fear—just foolish.

A man who is brave, steps through his fear, when he knows he must.

A wise man is one who knows when he must.

A truly functional man knows his fear is really only about change—the unknown. And, does this change merely concern the way he lives his life? Or is it about no longer living life?—because *that,* is the one kind of fear that may demand physical steps. The others only demand acceptance.

See Life's Laws:
3 Thoughts are energy: Loving, or not loving (fear).
17 What we hold with energy runs our life.
14 Change is the constant of the Universe.

Questions and/or Exercises:
- **Are you** one of the "foolish" brave people? Or, what is it you fear just now?
- **Is the** fear about some physical danger? Or about change to your life and your feelings about it?
- **What steps** do you need take to get through it? *And will you take them?*

You Are The Teacher

That higher part of your mind connected to God, creates everything you consciously, but mostly unconsciously, accept you are worthy of having.

That "mostly unconscious" part of your mind is taught by the lessons of what you think, say, and do in every experience you have. That *"do"* part is the truth of your thinking *expressed.* It is so often expressed unconsciously, like a reflex—*because you seldom pay conscious attention to your thinking.*

Make no mistake; The Law states that *Thoughts Create.* It is you, who are the teacher of your unconscious mind—and those unconscious reflex experiences show the truth of your thinking. Of those things you *"do"* so unconsciously? —Make a conscious effort to know the truth of the *"why,"* you do them. For those are the truths that keep you from having everything you want.

See Life's Laws:
1   I am the creator.
22   We consciously only feel our own feelings.
20   We are part of the energy that comprises God.

Questions and/or Exercises:
- **What did** you think, say, and do, so unconsciously today? Make a list.
- **Ask yourself** how well those things align with what you want—of the *who* you see yourself as being.
- **Unconsciously or** consciously you do create what you want. Those things you don't think match your conscious wants, what is the truth of why you did unconsciously want them?

Forgiveness—The Stupid Shit

People will always say and do those stupid-shit things that you think are wrong. Then you find yourself having to go through the process of *"forgiving."* Thing is, would you ever need to forgive them if *you* hadn't judged *them* as *wrong* in the first place?

Truth is, forgiveness is about changing your perception of *them*, and about *forgiving yourself* having been so *judgmental* and *unloving*.

This might be well remembered for the next time you start to judge another person. Then if you think you are forgiving *them*, you will know that *you are still in the grip of being judgmental.*

But hey! You will forever be caught in the cycle of judging people wrong, then having to forgive them. That is unless?—

Unless you can realize that right and wrong don't exist, except in someone's judgmental mind! And why would anyone want to have a judgmental mind? Why do *you* want to see someone as somehow *"wrong"*—unless it is your way of seeing yourself as *right*, and them, somehow *not as good as?* Do you think—hmmmm?

Ah, but let's cut through our own *stupid-shit* stuff. Let's look at it in the framework of those Spiritual Laws. You see, beyond all that, is the simple fact that they are merely offering you the chance to learn something—some lesson that your own soul feels you need to learn.

Yes, you and I just went through the process of peeling this particular onion. Can you see how going directly to the Spiritual Laws can cut through and avoid a lot of that "stupid-shit stuff" in your life?

See Life's Laws:
7   Blame is the abdication of responsibility.
9   Others are but a mirror for us to see ourselves.
18   Soul to soul pacts are made in the pre-existence.
10   The purpose of life is for those lessons.

Questions and/or Exercises:
- **Can you** see that *right and wrong—good and bad* are a dysfunctional way of judging others? Why?
- **Could** *loving or unloving* be a more functional way? Why?
- **Which way** did your religion teach you to judge?
- **Did your** religion also teach that it is the other person who needs your forgiveness? What do you think now?

Then there is Forgiveness— The Serious Shit

Yes, and then there are those things that people sometimes do that actually cause real harm to you or a loved one—things that are way beyond the *"dumb shit"* stuff that you simply don't like. These are the things that are extremely painful physically or mentally. Sure, the mental stuff is pain we take on ourselves, but often it is pain that is unavoidable, given we are all human.

Again, we are talking way beyond the stupid shit stuff we dislike— way beyond that into feelings of hatefulness and revenge. Now those kind of feelings are as chains, connecting us to that other person forever and draining our reserve of energy.

Like a vampire sucking upon your very soul, it will run your life until you break the chain. Then, is when it may help, to see that other person as *"less than."* When you can see that they are not worth the energy you are expending, it is so much easier to break that chain.

We are given the choice by the Creator to live in the energy of love or that energy that is not love, rather fear. That other person, is someone who lives in that fearful place where there is no love. It is through your pity, that the chain can be broken. Their soul is just as magnificent as your own, but what they are doing to it is undeniably something to be pitied.

Empathy is when you connect with another person through love. Pity is different, it is to disconnect yourself. We are all beings of energy, remember. To stay connected through love would still be draining to your soul. You don't *empathise,* you don't *forgive,* you *pity!*

The fact is, there are people in this world you *don't* want to be connected with energetically. Yes, it is a hard lesson to learn that sometimes to love yourself requires you consciously disconnect from someone else.

Once you have healed and are no longer holding any energy on it, *then* you will find that the Universe is in balance because you will accept that they are who they are, and that you have stopped wanting to change them—and you may have even found something about the situation, for which you are thankful.

Ah, but given this process is one way of getting through the pain, *I don't recommend it!* I have to admit, it is the "stupid shit" exercise in onion peeling way of going about—or around—it. Taking this one directly to the Laws is for the truly courageous. Not everyone is ready or willing to learn this lesson in courage.

Here is the hard truth. Life is about the lessons. If this was about something they did that harmed you physically, then let's hope you learned to avoid that in the future.

If it was something that caused you pain mentally, then take responsibility. *You are the creator of your life—you create every bit of the mental pain that is in it.* And remember: you are the one who has to feel it—they do not.

They did what they did. "Did"—past tense. You cannot change it, and you have not accepted it. When you refuse to accept what you cannot change, you guarantee yourself pain. Seeing them as someone not worth it and disconnecting your energy—is one way to ease the pain. Seeing them as someone to be pitied —is two. But to hit the jack-pot requires you to stop banging your head into that solid brick wall of un-acceptance —the one you won't admit is there. *It is, what it is.* If you don't want it running the rest of your life, then accept it and move on. Only then will you be open to finding the gift in the experience—there is one, you know?

--- — — — ---

See Life's Laws:
5   For every sorrowful thing, there exists the potential for equal joy. The Universe always balances.
17 What we hold with energy runs our life.
19 We are quintessentially, beings of energy.

Questions and/or Exercises:
- **Is there** someone in your life who has harmed you to such an extent? One who like a vampire, still sucks your energy?
- **Can you** see that it is not about them sucking, rather you spewing it at them?
- **Do you** have the courage to stop—to break the connection—and just accept?
- **Do you** have the wisdom to then look for the gift? *Again, there is one y'know?*
- **Or are** you choosing instead to be pissed at me for telling you this?

Little Flying Lizards

Often others label you as a coward when they see your fear. The truth is, you are not, until you, yourself, put on that label. Every human on the planet has fears. A fear is only an imaginary dragon in your mind. It generally starts as a little flying lizard sent by your higher self out of love, to caution and warn you of perceived danger. Then it is blown-up large, fed by your conscious mind using the winds of possibility. We believe ourselves cowards—those of us who won't walk the dragon, until it is once again, a little lizard.

See Life's Laws:
8   The world is not "out there"—it is "in here." *Only you can change your mind.*

Questions and/or Exercises:
- **Again, is** this dragon withering and dying for lack of being fed?
- **Or is it** growing stronger, gorging on the mental shit coming out the ass-end of your mind?

Tigers

Your fears are generally unfounded—only the imaginary dragons of your mind. Yet strongly emotional unpleasant feelings, are *always* tigers, and *never* imaginary. Yes, your feelings are real and can, and often will, devour you. What is not real, is that they are created by someone somewhere outside of your mind, and that they have to be tigers. *Only when you own them can they then become pussy cats.*

See Life's Laws:
7   **Blame is** the abdication of responsibility.
8   **The world** is not "out there"—it is "in here."
17   **What we** hold with energy runs our life.

Questions and/or Exercises:
- **It is much** better to pet that before it becomes a tiger. Staving off someone else's tiger with a chair is generally a losing proposition. Question is: When it concerns another person's feelings, who needs to do the petting? Hint: It is *not* you.
- **Flip side:** If they are your own feelings—NOW who needs to do the petting?
- **Guy, or girl**, if you are in a relationship and busy blaming your partner for your choice of bad feelings—well, that just makes you the fearful little pussy who refuses to own that responsibility. My question to you—*ownerless pussy*—is: How long do you think it will be before your raging tiger consumes the relationship?

Feeding Frenzy

Feeding sharks or hearts; what's the difference? —They both are hungry. Sometimes both go into a feeding frenzy. Perhaps it's only that a loving heart won't take your arm off—not while living in the space of love.

Although there are those who might feel the shark is the better deal; given some hearts live in the energy of *fear* rather than *love*. And clearly, that would be a heart to which one knows better than to get too close. *A heart that vacillates between love and fear, is the one most likely to bite you---and it will be in your behind.*

See Life's Laws:
3   Thoughts are energy: Loving, or not loving (fear).
8   The world is not "out there"—it is "in here."
17   What we hold with energy runs our life.

Questions and/or Exercises:
- **Do you** think you can ever be close in your relationship if yours is a heart that vacillates?
- **Ladies, do** you feel your man is just chumming your shark, feeding you what they think you want to hear? You might want to reign in that shark?—and address your man only with your love, never your fear. *What do you think?*
- **And guys,** it's not just the ladies getting lied to by the men, but the reason both might lie is likely the same. Could it be that both are afraid of getting bit by the other's shark—that the cost of telling the truth will be a chunk out of your ass?
- **The only** thing that *feeds* a relationship is love. Why would you ever vacillate it into fear—don't you know, fear *feeds on* your relationship? *Write down your thoughts about it.*

One's Way of Life

Sometimes with the death of one's old way of life, there remains a restless spirit—a spirit unable to sleep until it can say goodbye to all it has loved who are no longer part of the new. Such spirits reside in each of us, and to have rest in the new life, one must bring them to a loving completion.

Such a completion is called acceptance. It is you, accepting that person you loved, being exactly who they are. And you recognizing that it was you, making them wrong, and you, now forgiving yourself. *Your forgiveness is never about anyone but yourself.*

See Life's Laws:
17   What we hold with energy runs our life.

Questions and/or Exercises:
- **It was** with purpose, that I did not put this reflection in close proximity to the ones on forgiveness. Why do you think that is?
- **In repeating** the same concept, but in a different way, it's true one may hear and accept only one. Of those who understood it all, does repeating it dilute its meaning? Or is this thought more about the death of one's old way of life, and not-so-much about forgiveness?
- **What if** reading this book would cause the death of your current way of life? Would you continue reading it? *Change your mind, change your life*—Y'know?

About Song

Song is the voice's connection to the soul–to all that personal "God the Creator" power. Even ancient man knew this. Perhaps modern man has just forgotten—it seems he now uses it for frivolous things. Just look at the lyrics of some popular songs . . .

How many are uplifting to the soul? With those that are—then is when we can feel our soul take flight. But with those that aren't—

——————— — — — ———————

See Life's Laws:
19   We are quintessentially, beings of energy.
3   Thoughts are energy: Loving, or not loving (fear).

Questions and/or Exercises:
- **The tune** may be catchy, but do the words—the sentiments—uplift your soul? *List some that do for you.*
- **Songs expressing** sentiments of revenge—can you see that they only validate someone who sees them self as a victim? Do such songs validate you?
- **Me? I'm just** a redneck, remember? And I dearly love my ". . . pretty little souped-up four wheel drive."—Know that song? *Write about the sentiments it suggests. Do they uplift you?*

Courage

Again, courage is not about facing death; it is about living life while facing fear. Courage is always preceded by the fear, normally of things that haven't yet happened. It might be wise to remember that with the energy of that fear itself, we are busy creating, or attracting into our lives, the very thing we fear—right now.

See Life's Laws:
2   Thoughts create.
3   Thoughts are energy: Loving, or not loving (fear).
24   What we dwell upon with energy—is what we attract.

Questions and/or Exercises:
- Do you remember the Law: **Whatever our thoughts dwell upon with energy is what we are attracting into our life right now?** What are the things you most fear right now?
- **Do you** really want to create your life to be exactly what you *don't* want?
- **Do you** now see how important it is to face life with courage? *Write about it.*

Earning Respect

Do you think that with those folks who demand you earn their respect, it is because they feel that giving respect somehow takes something away from themselves—something they're too socially and emotionally cheap to give. Maybe so—

But could the real truth be, it is only about getting control. If you jump through their hoops long enough, they may decide they like you. But respect you? —Not a chance. Such people are not givers of respect; they're takers of your energy.

See Life's Laws:
19   We are quintessentially, beings of energy.
7   Blame is the abdication of responsibility.

Questions and/or Exercises:
- **Are there** people in your life, whose respect you want, but don't feel you get? *List them.*
- **Have you** ever felt depleted just by being around them? *Write about it.*
- **Do you** not see that control is a fallacy, but that the energy they suck from you in the effort to control, is not? *Note down your thoughts on all of it.*

Needs and Wants

There are physical needs that sometimes require the help of others to sustain your body. But the mental—those also often require the help of someone else, but only to make you aware of those needs. But the meeting of them always, requires only you. No one who knows them self is ever needy. Because knowing yourself, is the only true mental need, there is.

And wants? Only when your needs are met can you deal with wants. Until then, the needs, consciously or unconsciously, run your life.

The Universe/God gives us everything we need. With the mental needs, help usually comes in the form of a "significant other," who will stir up your life and help you get to know yourself—mirrors, remember?

Once you've done your part, then your relationships will never again be needy. They then become about someone you simply want to be with, someone you will accept exactly as they are. And maybe—just maybe—in light of your example, they will do the same.

See Life's Laws:
9   Others are but a mirror for us to see ourselves.
8   The world is not "out there"—it is "in here."
12   Our lives are run first by our needs—then our wants.
18   Soul to soul pacts are made in the pre-existence.

Questions and/or Exercises:
- **Of the** needs we are talking about here?—Those physical are about sustaining your life. The mental—those are the true needs of your soul. *Write about it.*
- **Why do** you think that is?
- **Could it be** that it is the experience of it—of knowing yourself in this physical life—that, is what your soul craves?
- **Would that** then mean. that the reason you are here in life, is to gain the experience your soul needs to grow and evolve? *Keep writing—keep breathing.*

My Viewpoint— In Redneck Speak

You know how a new swimmer tries to throw their head back, to keep their mouth and nose above the water at all times? Eventually, most will give that up and just accept, that sometimes it's necessary to just close their mouth to the reality of it occasionally being under the surface. Now that is functional. And then sometimes, there are those who just won't.

They are the ones who go through life with their head kinked back to hold their mouth and nose up out of the realities of being human. Are they afraid someone might've pissed in the pool?

Could it be that they *know* someone has—from personal experience?

Even so, with their mouth held above the pissy waters of humanity, it is always free to tell others what they "should" do—and also to take offense when they don't. While it is nice to never need to shut ones mouth, or to keep opinions to ones self, it does create one big personal problem. It's hard to maintain that posture when it puts such a strain on the neck.

So, to make it easier on themselves, they use a stick as a prop to hold their heads up in that superior position. And the only way to do that, is to insert that stick up their butt.

Then there's the problem that they just can't see, what with their viewpoint is always looking at something loftier than everyone else's. Makes it hard for them to see that no one likes or appreciates them. It's only when they find someone whom they themselves like, that their stick then becomes just a little too uncomfortable. Rather than take responsibility, it's just easier to blame, and to take offense at things, that were never meant to be offensive. Yes, it is a heartbreaking thing when one keeps running those, whom they've come to care about, right out of their lives—and can't see why.

But hey, their field of view doesn't allow them to see. About the only thing that will, is when someone comes along who cares enough to give that stick a good tug. A stick like that likely has become such a part of their person, that they've forgotten it being there. But a stick like that is a dangerous thing, if someone were to just jerk it out. After the ensuing explosion, that stick will just be put back in its uncomfortable, but familiar place—such a dysfunctional crutch.

The fact is, no one has the right to remove another's stick. And it is such a rare—even stellar—occurrence, when a person has the courage to deal with the humiliating experience of pulling their stick out and exposing what has really been inside—how that stick has been keeping their shit from stinking for so long. The only way it can even be done, is by rejecting the reason that stick was installed in the first place—that is, by being themselves, and not giving a shit about what other people think.

Bottom line: Isn't that what that whole "nose-in-the-air" facade, was all about in the first place—them wanting others to think they were "better than?" Seems to me that they could do with a little "essence of redneck."

But hey—I'm just a redneck. One who "don't-give-a-shit-what-you-think" simply because he doesn't need to be better than you, to like who he is.
No—this redneck
"don . . . neeed . . . no . . . steeen–king . . . steeeck,"
just to like himself.

——— — — — ———

See Life's Laws:
8   The world is not "out there"—it is "in here."
17   What we hold with energy runs our life.
7   Blame is the abdication of responsibility.

Questions and/or Exercises:
- **Can you** see that the whole thing is summed up by that one phrase: by. . . "don't-give-a-shit-what-you-think." Do you think that's a negative thing?
- **What if** "negative and positive" were also just an expression of your personal judgments—like "right and wrong?"
- **Is running** your life in fear of what other people will think, a positive thing? What do you think?
- **And that** stick mentioned?—Could be it's just a simile for "better than?"
- **If you've** got one, I suspect you now know it. I just gave it a loving little tug. *Y'know?*

About Offensive People

There are mean-spirited acts, and there are acts of good will. Both are of equal service in determining with whom I want to associate.

So, when by their actions, someone is showing me the meanness of their spirit—and assuming there is no personal threat—why would I want to take offense? Aren't they doing me a service?

See Life's Laws:
8   The world is not "out there"—it is "in here."
19   We are quintessentially, beings of energy.
3   Thoughts are energy: Loving, or not loving (fear).

Questions and/or Exercises:
- **Do you** agree that "perception is a choice?"
- **Do you** see that your feelings are also a choice?
- **In the** choice of your perception, and/or your feelings, what changes could you make that would better serve you in life?

PART THREE
Reflections of Love
In the Light of the Laws

Unconditional Love

In a relationship where there is unconditional love, there is also ultimate freedom. That is what loving unconditionally means. Each has the inalienable right to be exactly who they are and still be loved and accepted. No one ever pays a price for honesty.

Got dishonesty in your relationship? —Maybe you need to look for where your love may be conditional.

See Life's Laws:
21 Real love, once given, cannot be taken back.
13 Our own life is our sole possession. Just so, it is for everyone.

Questions and/or Exercises:
- **Do you** get that real love is always unconditional/ What conditions have you placed on your own love? *Write about it.*
- **If yours** is unconditional, but theirs isn't, are you willing to be their teacher?
- **Can you** accept that they may not learn? If you can't—then you gotta know: *Your love is still conditional.*

Accepting

I hear people complaining about their significant others and often want to tell them the hard truth that they don't want to hear. It is only with the rare one, who asks that I speak. Most people have to be drowning before they will reach out for what they need. Some even prefer to drown, rather than face the truth about themselves.

And the truth about you and me? —The simple truth is, we don't have the right to jump into anyone's life without being invited. And even then, neither of us is so above another that we can save them.

The fact that you are reading this book, I consider to be your invitation for me to speak. Still, this book is a waste of your time if you don't want something better in life. *And I would have to accept that about you.* If I didn't, it would not be because you aren't acceptable. Again, it would be about me not accepting you.

So now, I started out talking about relationships . . .

If you are unhappy with your significant other, then the relationship is a waste of time for you both—*If,* you don't want to change *"you"* to make it better. If you do, then consider; it is not because she (or he) is not acceptable, being exactly who they are. Yes, you've got it; it is because *you* aren't accepting of *them.*

Your life is not about anyone but you. That they are in your life, is only because they were sent by a higher power, to point out every unlovable thing there is about you. Those things that could make you a better person; were you to just look at, and truly own them—and sometimes, change.

Are they really unlovable—or are you just unloving?

See Life's Laws:
9   Others are but a mirror for us to see ourselves.
8   The world is not "out there"—it is "in here."
18   Soul to soul pacts are made in the pre-existence.
10   The purpose of life is for those lessons.
13   Our own life is our sole possession. Just so, it is for everyone.

Questions and/or Exercises:
- **There are** four basic messages here. *List what you think they are. If you think you may have missed something, come back after you have finished this book and do this one again.*
- **Is there** anything about these simple messages you cannot accept? If so, turn back to Part Two and read Law 7. *Then write about what you then see. These questions and exercises are deliberately vague because the understandings here are critical, to having a successful relationship. I can't save you, neither can this book. But it can be a **floatation devise for you to save yourself.***

About Relationships

What does it take to make a good relationship between a person and their mate? I'd have to say safety and honesty.

That is, safety both physically and emotionally. Each must know the other would never harm them physically or reject them emotionally—no matter what.

And honesty?—Honesty is a much stickier matter. Knowing we have that emotional safety—that you will never be made to pay an emotional price for your honesty with me, requires we both be willing to search within, for the truth about our feelings. Why am I feeling angry/sad/upset about what you have said or done? I must understand and deal with my own feelings—*but mainly, I must own them.* Only when I can deal with you without blame, can we—either one—truly have anything that approaches honesty.

I know, sounds pretty esoteric. In the *"real world,"* it is just so much easier to make them pay for *your choice* of feelings—Yeah, in that world, *they're going to pay!* But then so will you. You surely don't expect them to be honest with you, when the only way they can avoid your revenge, is to tell you the lie you want to hear.

See Life's Laws:
7 Blame is the abdication of responsibility.
8 The world is not "out there"—it is "in here."

Questions and/or Exercises:
- **Have you** ever had a significant other lie to you?
- **Do you** now understand why? *Explain.*

Odd Thoughts

Something I've learned about relationships:

Growing or dying, life never stops and takes a breath. It's always changing, always heading somewhere. If you both don't have the same place in mind somewhere down the road —you just don't get there together.

See Life's Laws:
14   Change is the constant of the Universe.
8   The world is not "out there"—it is "in here."
13   Our own life is our sole possession. Just so, it is for everyone.

Questions and/or Exercises:
- **Have you** discussed with your significant other exactly where it is you want to go in life?
- **Is it the** same place? *Write about it.*
- **If you haven't**, *don't you think you might want to give them a heads-up on this one?*

The Truth About Commitment

Relationships are a constant balancing act—balancing what one receives from the relationship with what one gives. The moment one side of the scale slams full-up, it's inevitable that someone will fall off. Sustaining the balance is always a two party effort. For the balance is a touchy thing. Is what you are giving, what they may want to receive? Maybe it is you who won't accept—receive—what they are giving? And maybe one is just too stingy with their love?—We are talking about love here—giving and receiving it in the way we want it—y'know. In the end it only takes one to part. And it matters not if that one simply gets off or falls off.

And parting?—It is not always a physical thing. Some will claim commitment and choose to stay together. They are the liars in life. For this is your own life and it cannot be given away to another, not without being dishonest to your soul. *Commitment can only be to one's self in one's own life—Commitment to someone else is always a lie!*

It is a lie you tell first to your own soul, and then to the other's. It is told because it supports your greatest fear—

the fear that you aren't loveable. The fear that you—or they—won't be able to hold, or be worthy of the other's love.

Staying with someone you no longer love, is an even more insidious lie. Real love, once given can never be taken back. If you no longer love them, then the truth is, *you never loved them at all.* Real love or not, relationships require the balance.

Relationships are always about meeting one another's needs. Only the really great ones involve real love. The others? —The others are simply based on fear. One can recognize them by the demands for commitment—the promises in those lies—and then all the drama and the struggle for control that inevitably follows.

The needs are about balancing the love remember, not the about balancing your fears. Bottom line: relationships provide the perfect place and the perfect person to give you the lessons in life you need to grow past your fears, and learn to love. The trick is that when you fall off that horse, get back on. You may be in for a few rough rides, and it could take a whole heard of horses, but eventually, you will learn to love.

——— — — — ———

See Life's Laws:
21   Real love, once given, cannot be taken back.
13   Our own life is our sole possession. Just so, it is for everyone.
12   Our lives are run by our needs—then our wants.
10   The purpose of life is for those lessons.

Questions and/or Exercises:
- **Do you stay** because you want to, or because of some lie called commitment?
- **Have you the** courage to love without assurance—the "courage" part, requires you to chance they may not feel the same way, y'know?
- **If your** relationship's over, and there are hard feelings, be sure they are not yours. Only then can your next one be someone you love—indeed, have you learned how to love? *Write about that one.*

About Proving One's Love

If you want your mate to prove their love—or to fight for your own—you are not a person going about the business of *love,* rather you are going about the business of *control.* You are not a person *"in love."* You are a person *"in fear."* Perhaps most of all, your fear is that someday your mate will see this truth.

And truth? —Truth is, they will never win your love. Nor will you win control. Both are things that have to be given.

Might be wise to consider; control can be taken back, but real love, once given, is never taken back. Real love cannot be given, or accepted, by someone who is just concerned with a fearful need to control.

--- — — — ---

See Life's Laws:
3   Thoughts are energy: Loving, or not loving (fear).
16   We only control ourselves.
21   Real love, once given, cannot be taken back.

Questions and/or Exercises:
- **Do you** see that with love, there is no ***fighting***, there is no ***winning***—there is only ***accepting?***
- **Do you** have the courage not to fear love?—You do know that there cannot be love, if there is fear—don't you? If you have a grasp on these Laws of Life—then this answer will be clear. *If not, re-read the above laws—the long form—in Part Two. Then write about it*

Magnets

Everyone has a personal magnet. Most insist on marking the opposite ends as *right and wrong*. Yet such labels do in fact, have no real meaning, as they are never exactly the same in anyone else's mind. Why not label with, what is truth in every heart?—Things that sustain one's soul and things that don't.

Yes, the poles are clear when marked only *love* and *fear*. Being human, I am the magnet: a curious mixture of both. Being aware, I know from which end I want to attract. Do the chameleons called *right and wrong,* really give one that possibility? Is the truth not really, that however mislabeled, our magnets are the same? It's just that being "right," keeps some from being "aware." Aware perhaps, that their "right," often is really just the side of fear—and perhaps so "fearfully right" they cannot hear. And perhaps I'm only talking to dead air—perhaps.

With someone you love, that possibility is so hard to bear. And sometimes, we simply must let go: reach out instead, and touch those who love—those who will touch back—and nurture our souls with acceptance.

See Life's Laws:
3   Thoughts are energy: Loving, or not loving (fear).
4   The energy out, returns in kind.
5   For every sorrowful thing, there exists the potential for equal joy. The Universe always balances.

Questions and/or Exercises:
- **Is "right and wrong"** ultimately the peak for a mountain of dung dribbling out of the back end of a judgmental mind?
- **Speaking of** "dead air"—if your mind is locked into "right and wrong", the air around this last question won't be smelling very pleasant. So, is it?
- **If you do** smell the stink, don't you think you owe it to your soul, to search out the thoughts and beliefs that are its source and change them?

The Truth about Love

The need to feel loved is a basic human need. It is a need that cannot be filled outside one's self. Yet virtually all of Humanity has this need, for virtually no one has been taught to love them self—and to put that love before all others.

To be humble in our society is an admirable thing. *We are taught* to look at ourselves as less than, and certainly not equal to others. *We are taught* to sacrifice ourselves, because others are better and more deserving. *We are taught* to believe that our own life is not as worthy as another's.

Bottom line, *we are taught to be dysfunctional.* The truth is, we can only feel our own love. And without ever having felt it for ourselves, can we truly know love? No—nor can we have it to give to others. It is not that we need to feel loved, it is that we need to love ourselves, and then to feel ourselves loving others—and sometimes, to know that our love is returned.

See Life's Laws:
4   The energy out, returns in kind.
22   We consciously only feel our own feelings.
12   Our lives are run by our needs—then our wants.
15   One must do one's own thinking.
6   The energy of thoughts must flow.

Questions and/or Exercises:
- **Is love** an ego thing? Can it in any way, be connected to the ego?
- **Is it** about being "better than?" Or is it just about "being?"
- **Is "being love"** something you have ever felt for yourself?
- **If not**—don't you know, you've yet to feel it for another? *Don't just answer "yes" or "no" here—write about it. And about how you feel about all those lies you have been taught.*

The Journey of the Heart

Commitment is only functional when it is to yourself. You *don't* know if you will always be with that other person, should there come a time when you—or they—don't want to be. You *do* know you will always be with yourself. The commitment part in about you loving you.

It is to commit to following your joy in life, and when you are with someone else, to loving them to the very best of your ability.

And if sometime those joys should vary, and your paths depart, be committed to letting them go with love. It matters not what the other does, it is up to each to part with love—or not. This is when you each get to discover if your own love for them is real—and if theirs is also.

Commitment to love and to joy—to following your heart—is a personal journey. Your travel companions may change. But the love in your heart will not. If you loved them then, you will love them always—love is a forever thing.

Did you part with love—and did they? Perhaps they were in your life to give you this lesson about love—to show you if your love is the real deal. Maybe this is a lesson you gave to one another. The only things you need to consider are: Did *you* learn the lesson—did *you* learn how to love?

***

See Life's Laws:
21   Real love, once given, cannot be taken back.
10   The purpose of life is for those lessons.
8   The world is not "out there"—it is "in here."
18   Soul to soul pacts are made in the pre-existence.

Questions and/or Exercises:
- **If anyone** had hard-feeling on parting, what does that tell you about them?
- **Was it** you?
- **Can real** love for you, ever depend on them doing, saying, or being, anything other than they are?
- **If you** don't know within yourself what real love is, how can you ever know it, or accept it, when it is being given?

Living to Our Joy

If my mate won't live life to the joys that are hers alone, regardless of what I or others want, she's not living true to herself. If her life is a lie unto herself, how can it ever be otherwise to me? A lie is a lie. If it is something she says by way of convincing herself, the lie will show up expressed to me. Inside she knows, and her life cannot go for long without expressing the truth.

Our true thoughts cannot help but create. It is a Spiritual Law: Thoughts create—always.

Wouldn't it be best to just live our lives to our own joys, restricting only those which are harmful to ourselves or others, in actuality—being aware of our own ego and ignoring the egos of others? Anyone whose ego is a stumbling block in my life, doesn't belong there. For I give them this same courtesy.

My feelings are the messages from my soul, sent to tell me what I need to look at, in order to grow. It is not my right to save others from their own feelings—from their own learning. And, I do consider it my duty, to be honest with others about who I am.

Again, those who run their lives to suit their ego and expect us to run ours, to suit that same ego, don't belong in our lives—those of us who want to live in truth.

Sometimes that is a bitter truth to accept, when it is about the person you love.

Still . . . A lie is a lie. The ego is the master of all liars. To become a liar, just to masturbate your loved one's ego—to make it feel good—where is there any love in that?

———— — — — ————

See Life's Laws:
2   Thoughts Create.
13   Our own life is our sole possession. Just so, it is for everyone.

Questions and/or Exercises:
- **Requiring** your mate to masturbate your ego may seem like fun. But the ensuing orgasm will make your relationship very sticky. Have you experienced it? *Write about it.*
- **There are** those who play the game of control and think it is love. Is this the bitter truth about the one you love? *Write about it—truthfully.*
- **Do you** understand that it is a demand they make of you, if you are to be allowed in their life?
- **Do you** know that to give in to that demand, is to make a death wish to your soul? *Why is that?*

I'm Okay...

"*I'm okay—you're all fucked-up*" Such seems to be the lowest common denominator in the minds of many. "*In my life, I am better than you!*"

Perhaps we, in all our relationships, simply need to take another step in conscious evolution.

"*I'm okay—for me. You're okay—for you. And, I see the love in you.*"

See Life's Laws:
13   Our own life is our sole possession. Just so, it is for everyone.
19   We are quintessentially, beings of energy.
4   The energy out, returns in kind.

Questions and/or Exercises:
- **It's none of** your business if others see you as "fucked-up." Only when you can accept it is their right—and not give a rats-ass—will they then have the opportunity to freely change their minds. *Surely you know someone who views you that way. Will you try it sincerely, in-no-way making it into a game of pretense.*
- **If that person** is your significant, can you accept that you may be the only one in the relationship who evolves?

The Other Half of Loving is Accepting

A relationship is really only about needs and learning. Each person getting their own needs met, and each learning about themselves, in this great mirror called relationship. When the relationship is especially good, the needs met, include the need to love. The learning in the mirror reflects the beauty of it. Yet for each, the relationship provides only the opportunity. It is about more than the giving, for each must also be willing to accept, and all in the space of honesty.

See Life's Laws:
9   Others are but a mirror for us to see ourselves.
6   The energy of thoughts must flow.

Questions and/or Exercises:
- **Is there** any need you have, that you are afraid to express to your partner?
- **Are you** aware that it will bite you in the ass if you don't? **Write about it.**
- **Do you** know that if you are "afraid", it is because you don't feel safe to be real and honest with them?
- **Do you** think they might have the same issues with you, about their own needs?
- **How can** you make your relationship a safe place for them to be?

Love and Acceptance

Love means a lot of different things, to a lot of different people. But the bottom-line real truth about love is that it requires acceptance. It is a total thing—an all-out or nothing thing. This is why it requires acceptance.

Without acceptance, love is not love. It is simply need
- the need for someone to be other than who they are with you.
- the need to control other people, because they are responsible for how we feel about ourselves.
- the need for you to believe in other people, because you don't believe in yourself.
- the need for you to look outside yourself, for someone who cares.
- the need for you to have someone else fill those gaps in you, where you are not there.

Yes, without acceptance, there is simply need. Yet with acceptance there is still a need—a need to give love. Real love is a giving thing, needing nothing outside of its giving.

See Life's Laws:
8   The world is not "out there"—it is "in here."
6   The energy of thoughts must flow.
13   Our own life is our sole possession. Just so, it is for everyone.
21   Real love, once given, cannot be taken back.

Questions and/or Exercises:
- **Do you** see that without acceptance, what most then see as being love, is only fear?
- **And those** needs mentioned?—Might they be the lies society has taught you to believe?

Driving a Relationship

Relationships are about the lessons. What drives them are your needs. For some, the relationship may have nothing to do with love.

But likely, most would agree; relationships are supposed to be about the need to give and receive love. Yet no matter what the needs may be, for relationships to work, the meeting of needs must exist for both.

For when one's needs aren't met, they become the driving force in that person's life—the force that drives the relationship apart.

See Life's Laws:
12   Our lives are run by our needs—then our wants.

Questions and/or Exercises:
- **Is there** a force driving your relationship apart? If you don't know, then assume there is.
- **Is your** relationship a safe place for your partner to discuss his or her needs openly?
- **Do you** know that making it a safe place for you, requires you first make it so for them? *Write about it.*

Control Is Never Love

Having the courage to choose love in the face of that which is not, commands one's own respect.

That others cannot see it—others who would rather play that game of trying to control one another—others who would then try to convince themselves, by calling it love.

Yes, refusing to play that game takes courage, knowing you may no longer be accepted by those you love. And still, the fact remains, that playing the game of control with someone you "love"—is *never* loving.

See Life's Laws:
3   Thoughts are energy: Loving, or not loving (fear).
16   We only control ourselves.

Questions and/or Exercises:
- **How does** control raise its ugly little head in your own relationship?
- **Does it** too, spit at you if you don't submit—and doubly so, when you do?
- **Does it** show up as screaming-mee-mee fits of outrage—or just little insinuations of guilt?
- **In what** other ways has the game of control been played with you?—Or by you?

Giving

When you give of yourself—your love—to someone else, you are the one who gets the gift. You are the one who gets to feel your feelings.

***

See Life's Laws:
6   The energy of thoughts must flow.
22   We consciously only feel our own feelings.

Questions and/or Exercises:
- **Do you** feel it to be a special thing to love someone who accepts your love?
- **Is it then** required that they love you back?
- **If they** won't, would you still love them? This question especially, will tell you loads about yourself and love—*don't screw yourself with a "yes" or "no" answer.*

No Freedom—No Love

For me, I don't ever want to be in a relationship again where the lady is only staying because she feels she is stuck there by her marriage vows.

I want it to be that every time I look at her, I know that being with me is truly where she wants to be.

Let that bird free! Real love is to give one another that freedom.

Sure, I see things differently. To me, there is NO security in life. And yet, there are many who don't see it that way and spend a great deal of effort seeking it. I don't begrudge them their right to the illusive security of that false belief.

See Life's Laws:
8   The world is not "out there"—it is "in here."
3   Thoughts are energy: Loving, or not loving (fear).
16   We only control ourselves.

Questions and/or Exercises:
- **Do you** get, that by making any demands on how you want another to be, guarantees they won't show you the truth of who they are?
- **Would you** ever be okay with your significant other being with you, if they don't want to be?
- **How can** you ever know, if you try to control them in any way?
- **The only** thing that restricts freedom in your relationships, is found in any price you might demand they pay. Do you see the need to make your relationship a "free to be yourself" place? *Write about it.*

The Way You Want It

For a love to flourish, each must communicate, each must nourish. Each must be willing to look at—understand and fulfill—the needs of the other. Yes, everyone has a belief system about love. Mine is not the same as yours. The trick is, for me to tell you mine and to hear yours—then to give my love to you, in the way you want it.

If I cannot do that within the honest bounds of the joys of my soul, then it needs be, that I take the lessons of you—the lessons of us—and move on.

And you? —We are each in this world with our own life to live. What lessons you accept of me, are those you *want* to see—or maybe *need* to see—given you have the courage to look at all the private things I've told you. And I, to look at those things that are equally private to you, as mine are to me.

See Life's Laws:
9   Others are but a mirror for us to see ourselves.
18   Soul to soul pacts are made in the pre-existence.
12   Our lives are run by our needs—then our wants.
13   Our own life is our sole possession. Just so, it is for everyone.

Questions and/or Exercises:
- ➤ **". . . those things that are equally private to you, as mine are to me."** Can you see that this is the whole crux of love/sexual relationships? They are about private things—things exposed and vulnerable!
- ➤ **You might** not have even understood it when you read it above. Did you?
- ➤ **It is** the reason I am going over this material repeatedly in different scenarios. Unless it is something dead-on personal, exactly like it is in their own life, some folks can't see it. Y'know?
- ➤ **The concept** about what real love is, may be simple—the lies some folks tell about what they think love is, are often complex. Can you see that? *Yup, you got it—write about it.*

Ultimatums

An ultimatum is the Hiroshima of control dramas. It is one person demanding the other to be different than they are, in order to be acceptable. It is one saying, "I don't accept you being you." And a control drama, like all dramas, it is not love. So that person is also saying, "I don't love you."

Yeah, that one hits you like an nuclear bomb, doesn't it?

Ultimatums seldom sneak-up on you like an unexpected fart. Unless a person is one hell of a control freak, they will never give you an ultimatum—not without repeatedly letting you know exactly what it is about you, that is unacceptable to them. An ultimatum is the ultimate in the selfish pursuit, of trying to change you to suit them.

The fall-out from an ultimatum is deadly to a relationship.

See Life's Laws:
3   Thoughts Are Energy: *Love*, or *not love (fear)*
13   Our Own Life Is Our Sole Possession. Just So, It Is For Everyone.
16   We Only Control Ourselves.
21   Real Love, Once Given, Cannot Be Taken Back
26   Change Requires The Truth of One's Heart.

Questions and/or Exercises:
- **If you** truly wanted to be this person they are demanding you to be, wouldn't you have already become that person?
- **Can you** see, that for you, to make an unwanted change for them, would be to live a lie—an unsustainable lie?
- **Do you** really want to become a liar, pretending to be someone they can pretend to love?
- **Do you** want a relationship based on a struggle to control, or one based on love?
- **Isn't it** clear, you can't have both? *Write down your thoughts— don't wimp-out on yourself with yes or no answers.*

The Relationship Game

If you don't like the games being played in your relationship—the drama—the control . . .

Then you must become aware that you are in the game—and that control is never love, rather, always fear. You are playing your own part in it—and you can stop. Then the relationship will either stop—or change. You are the creator of the game you play—or don't play.

Most continue to play, only out of fear of what they will lose if they stop. Never being aware of the love one gains in not playing the game of control, and in having a relationship with a person also, not playing.

Will that person be the same person you are playing with now? That depends on if they are more enamored with the fearful illusion of control—something they currently are very familiar with—or, if they have the capacity to change to something they do not know: *real love*.

See Life's Laws:
13   Our own life is our sole possession. Just so, it is for everyone.
3   Thoughts are energy: Loving, or not loving (fear).
4   The energy out, returns in kind.
5   For every sorrowful thing, there exists the potential for equal joy. The Universe always balances.

Questions and/or Exercises:
- **The only** question you truly have the right to consider is: Do **you** have that capacity?
- **Have you** been following—do you understand the concept yet of what real love is—or would you rather play the game of control?
- **If so,** what part in the game do you play? *What do you think about all this?*

Giving and Accepting

Your life is not about anyone but yourself—and then, there are relationships. That is where stuff gets really fuzzy. It might help to remember this: It is not what your mate gives to the relationship, rather what you accept from it, that is most often the limiting factor—for you.

To grow your life in a relationship, both must give and both must accept. You may do your life together, but it is still about yourself. You're just adding the option of loving someone else.

See Life's Laws:
13   Our own life is our sole possession. Just so, it is for everyone.
19   We are quintessentially, beings of energy.
22   We consciously only feel our own feelings.

Questions and/or Exercises:
- **Does your** significant other give you the option of loving him or her?
- **Do you** accept love from him or her?
- **Can you** see that a loving relationship cannot exist, if both parties won't give as well as receive?
- **Why do** you think I use the term "won't" instead of "can't?" *(Can't give a one-word answer here, can you? And no, the "f-bomb" is two words. Maybe it ought to be, but it doesn't stand for "fun bomb)." It's okay. I know, about all this ooey-gooey—heart on your sleeve, talk about your real feelings stuff. A lot of folks won't handle it. Yup. There I go with that "won't" shit again. The point here is to get real).*

Diamonds

It's really easy to love a diamond. But a diamond is still just a rock. How much does a rock love you back? Know of anyone you think of as being a diamond? Could it be that they too, are incapable of loving you back? —Or is it that you are incapable of seeing the beauty beyond the glitter?

Wow! That last thing gives a whole different take on why they might be incapable of loving you back—do you think?

Then again, you might ask yourself. "If it is only about glitter, can there be any real love going on here?"

See Life's Laws:
3   Thoughts are energy: Loving, or not loving (fear).
22   We consciously only feel our own feelings.
21   Real love, once given, cannot be taken back.

Questions and/or Exercises:
- **Well, IS** your relationship only about the glitter?
- **Do you** love them only for their looks?
- **Do you** think your own looks are what makes you loveable?
- **Or is the** glitter about how much money they—or you— have? ***Write about it.***

Relationships— Needs & Soul Mates

Relationships are simply about growing and providing one another with the lessons we need to grow, lessons that will be beat out—forged—over the anvil of our needs.

The difference between having a regular relationship or having that ultimate one, some call a "soul mate," is simply that soul mates don't go kicking and screaming when it comes to learning the lessons we provide for them.

As for that "anvil of your needs?" Soul mates won't break your anvil and go screaming into the night. Besides, your needs, are simply what it takes to know your own heart. With a soul mate, the learning is non-judgmental and easy.

And the rest? Everything else in life are just wants.

See Life's Laws:
8   The world is not "out there"—it is "in here."
7   Blame is the abdication of responsibility.
9   Others are but a mirror for us to see ourselves.
18   Soul to soul pacts are made in the pre-existence.
10   The purpose of life is for those lessons.
21   Real love, once given, cannot be taken back.

Questions and/or Exercises:
- **Do you** resist learning the lessons your mate provides?
- **Do you** ever try to change them rather than to accept the lesson?
- **Has either** one ever gone screaming into the night?
- **If so, was** it in search of someone who won't give you that lesson—or was it to crawl back at daybreak, asking for that same lesson all over again?
- **If any** of these questions apply to you, wouldn't it be easier to just learn the lesson? *Yep, write about it.*

Soul Mates

Love is being a companion.

Love is giving your companion the freedom to be exactly who they are, without penalty.

Love is in knowing there is nothing, for which you will need to forgive them. No matter what they do, you will always see the spiritual being they are, and love them.

Yes, you can always have a loving relationship, but the loving part must happen on your own side. It does not always happen equally on their side. Those things they do, may eventually become a deal-breaker for your relationship. Forgiving them, just means you accept them and don't hold them as being wrong in your own mind. It does not mean it works for you. If you truly love them, you will part with love, wishing them well and nothing less.

The truth is, you can love someone that you do not want to be with. And likely, it is only because your love is not being returned, in the same manner and measure it is given—the energy of your love does not match. You are not mentally and/or spiritually matched.

Spiritually? Love happens on a spiritual plane. Relationships happen on this, the physical plane. Soul mates happen only when these planes are a match for both. What most on this physical plane think of as love, is more likely to be fearful need.

And mentally? That's about the consciously physical plane. Let's take that answer to the extreme. If your partner wants to have sex with other people, that must be something you are okay with—if you are mentally matched. Tough order—finding someone with the kind of courage to be that honest. Even tougher for them to find someone with that kind of acceptance.

Funny thing, the last statistic I heard was that cheating covers about 60% of married men and 40% of wives. Too bad people cannot always be honest about their sexuality. The 20% of women left over would then have no valid excuse to blame anyone but themselves—and 40% of all men and women could be having a great time swinging. Of the 40% who are monogamously faithful, hopefully they will stay that way—or at least be honest if they don't. But then, maybe the 20% of those ladies pissed-off and divorced can then even up the score.

What does all this say about honesty? Can there be any question that dishonesty is the cock-blocker to everything "relationship?" Without honesty, one can never know who the other is. *You have nothing, if either of what you give and what you get, is not honest—double that nothing, if if it is the same with your partner.*

───── ─ ─ ─ ─────

See Life's Laws:
21   Real love, once given, cannot be taken back.
16   We only control ourselves.
22   We consciously only feel our own feelings.

Questions and/or Exercises:
- **I used** sex for the "mentally matched" example, because sex is where relationships get hung-up the most. Has cheating ever happened by you, or to you?
- **Are you** spiritually and mentally matched with your mate?
- **You cannot** know that if you both have not been honest—have you? Honesty starts with you.
- **Do you** have honesty in your relationship? That is not to say you or they, haven't made mistakes—which brings up the question of acceptance.
- **Are you** both free to be exactly who you are—ALWAYS? *Yes, there's a lot to write about here.*

Lovegasm

Unhealthy people fall in love to fill the emptiness—the missing needs that they mistake as somehow being not whole. They attempt to find someone *"out there"* to fill it, for the needs are most always about love. Healthy people, are those who have looked within themselves for the love they need, and finding it, filled themselves to overflowing. Once there is such an abundance on the inside, they then look to someone *"out there,"* for which to give it. When they find someone of equal abundance, only then can love blossom past simple need, to the full fruition of a "lovegasm."

See Life's Laws:
6   The energy of thoughts must flow.
8   The world is not "out there"—it is "in here."
12   Our lives are run first by our needs—then our wants.
3   Thoughts are energy: loving, or not loving (fear).

Questions and/or Exercises:
- **Do you** understand that this is the first step you take on the path to your soul mate?
- **Do you** believe that love begins from inside or outside ourselves?
- **Could those** described as "healthy" ever get that way except by choosing the energy of love in their daily life, instead of fear?
- **Perhaps the** real question you need answer here is: Given those as described above, where do you fit in—healthy or unhealthy? *Why?*

Work at a Relationship

It is not true that you have to "work at a relationship". You just have to work at the lessons—the lessons concerning you, that the other person is providing. Concentrating on the lessons is the hard part.

Learning to accept the other, *exactly as they are,* is always one of your hardest lessons. Much easier to focus on fixing and changing—that struggle to control one another.

See Life's Laws:
9   Others are but a mirror for us to see ourselves.
10   The purpose of life is for those lessons.
18   Soul to soul pacts are made in the pre-existence.

Questions and/or Exercises:
- **What does** the term "work at a relationship" mean to you?
- **Is it about** dealing with what you dislike about them—about trying to make compromises with each other, in order to be acceptable companions?
- **When each** has to change something about themselves that they don't want to change, can either have what they want?
- **Wouldn't it** then be a lose/lose situation?
- **You changing** your perception to seeing them as acceptable—exactly as they are—would that not help them to see you the same way?

A Single Man's Prayer

Lord save me from the "religious" woman! For if her God is the source for all joy in her life, guess who gets to be responsible for all her pain . . .

Thank you God for the power in the knowledge given by the Spiritual Law: "I am the Creator"—that *we* are *one* with the power of the Universe. And my connection with that power creates everything in my life.

Given a physical attraction, some special joys in common, and a woman who is also the sole creator of her life, then there is no limit to the joy we will create together, *one* with *You!*

Namaste' Lord . . . Namaste'.

--- — — — ---

See Life's Laws:
1   I am the creator.
20   We are part of the energy that comprises God.
7   Blame is the abdication of responsibility.

Questions and/or Exercises:
> **You would** have to accept and understand these "Laws of Life" in order to understand what this one is saying. Do you? If not, it's okay to come back at a later time and re-read. *The exercise here is to put this one in your own words.*

Fearful Needs

The experiencing of true love between two people never results in pain. Pain between lovers is always the direct result of fear—those unmet fearful needs within themselves!

See Life's Laws:
4   The energy out, returns in kind.
12   Our lives are run first by our needs—then our wants.
21   Real love, once given, cannot be taken back.

Questions and/or Exercises:
- **Is there** pain in your life because you loved someone and they left you?
- **If death** took them away, why is it that you can't honor them, by remembering them without the pain?
- **In fact**, no matter the reason they left, why is it you can't honor them with the joy of your love?
- **Honoring** someone who has left you, requires you to truly love them—love as in, then *and* now. True love, once given is forever. *Write down your thoughts on this.*

In the End

Love? It's not how you feel about someone you've just met, someone with whom you are starting a relationship. The *truth* is about how you feel when it has ended. Doesn't matter what has happened in the meantime—all that, doesn't mean *shit*. Fact is, if you don't love them and wish them the very best in the end, *then you never loved them at all.*

See Life's Laws:
21   Real love, once given, cannot be taken back.

Questions and/or Exercises:
- **Have you** ever had an ex who you now harbor harsh feelings toward?
- **If so,** wouldn't it be wise to think hard on this reflection?
- **It is** never too late to change your mind—not if you're still alive—y'know?
- ***Exercise: Let's look at what your needs were that drove your relationship.***
  Guys, ask yourselves: Were you just lonely and wanted some enjoyable sexual company?
  Did you need a servant—someone to keep the house clean, and cook, and wash the skid marks out of your shorts.
  Did you want someone who looked up to you and would put up with your shit?
  Now ladies ask yourselves: Was he only there to provide you security in life?
  Did you want to be one of his possessions?
  Did you need to have someone who appreciated the care you took of him?
  Now for you both: If one of you cheated, what was the need that the other wasn't meeting?

Perfect Love

Finding that one perfect love, is not about the perfection of that other person, rather the perfection of your own love.

See Life's Laws:
8 The world is not "out there"—it is "in here."
4 The energy out, returns in kind.
22 We consciously only feel our own feelings.

Questions and/or Exercises:
- **Do you** think that love is something that the other person gives to you—or is it something you give to them?
- **Given most** believe it is both, which one do you think you have control over?
- **Which one** do you not?
- **Is it possible** that the one you control, is the love that needs to be your sole concern? *Write about it.*

The Flashbulb of Love

When the flashbulb of fresh love goes off in your face, sometimes you trip over things in your way—things you don't see. Sometimes they are things you put there, then don't look at. Always, there is a dazzling haze left in the backlash of that flash, which hides the picture. You determine how long that haze will last. Some couples stumble through life in that haze together, forever. Others learn from the pain of their falls, look at their self-imposed obstacles, and gain the true gift of insight. With insight comes the ability to run, to move faster and further in one's life. Sometimes the gift is accepted by only one, whose heart then cries, as it is carried away by life.

See Life's Laws:
10 The purpose of life is for those lessons.
9 Others are but a mirror for us to see ourselves.
14 Change is the constant of the Universe.

Questions and/or Exercises:
- **Is it** possible that the other person was just in your life to teach you things about yourself?
- **Things that** for your soul to "know," you had to experience?
- **Can you** accept the "gift" of it and move on in life with gratitude?
- **Is it possible** it may not be the same experience for them?
- **That they** may not need this same "gift?"

Sex Is A Beautiful Thing

Let's talk the nitty-gritty about SEX—the physical act. Doesn't matter if it is love making—or FUCKING. Either way, it is a beautiful thing, and, as one ages, it WILL change.

Some women will lose their sexual "want to." Some men will lose their "ability to." I've heard it said that ED (erectile dysfunction) happens—to 70% of men at some point. I think that figure is lower than the truth.

I hope you women never have to face the following situation, but consider: some women get breast cancer and end up losing one or more breasts. Yes, assuming their survival, it is still a personal disaster—especially to their viewpoint of how they see themselves as a woman. It's no different to a man with ED. For BOTH, it is nothing short of a DISASTER!

And then, there is the bottom line of all sexual love—and all FUCKING. That being each person is giving the gift of it to the other, helping one another meet their need for sexual release. Women can take the hormones they may be lacking, and/or get their breasts rebuilt. A man can get toys—and too, develop his oral abilities.

But my point is that IT IS ALSO A GIFT when each is able to help the other see themselves as a functioning being again—yeah, maybe even a sexual dynamo.

Disaster? Hell, look to the up-side. A woman can have bigger perkier breast than she could otherwise—given the realities of aging. A man can give his woman a variety, or maybe just the exact size, shape, and feel of her preferred dick—and can make the act last throughout her ability to have multiple orgasms. That's not to mention, he can develop his taste buds for sexual cuisine. In the

process, EACH is given the gift of sex, AND, a gift concerning their personal viewpoint in how they view themselves as a sexual being.

Thing is, sex is a NEED. Something necessary to having and keeping one's body and/or mind healthy. If one or the other partner can't or won't—given you love them and want to be together—it all boils down to your feelings about it. And you have the power to change your feelings. If you are the one who can't or won't, wouldn't you want your partner to get their needs met? If you truly love them, you will. You can be okay encouraging them to get their sexual needs met in an open/honest manner, by someone who can or wants to. Yeah, that's right: it's called an "open" relationship, and it can work for you.

There are options in a changing—mature—relationship. YOU—each person reading this—can make those golden years even better sexually, than the BEST years you ever had while moaning with those raging hormones of youth—given you want to.

See Life's Laws:
1   I am the creator.
5   For every sorrowful thing, there exists the potential for equal joy. The Universe always balances.
8   The world is not "out there"—it is "in here."

Questions and/or exercises:
- **If sex is** an issue, will you approach your partner for an honest solution?
- **If he can't** as a man, as a woman, can you accept alternatives to the reality of "man-meat—possibly even enjoy the alternatives more?"
- **If you** have a problem with either of the above questions, is it possible you have love and ego mixed?
- **Man or** woman, do you now look at aging and sexuality differently?
- *Write about your thoughts, personal experiences, and/or intensions about this.*

In the Energy

In the energy of life there is only *love* or what is not love —*fear*. (Yeah, I'm still harping on law 3).

To be in a relationship, just because both want to be there—that's about *love*. And it's also about *freedom,* as either has the freedom to *not* be together, if it's not where they want to be.

To have a relationship where either one demands promises or legal chains, that's *not* love—not the pure freedom of *love*—rather that's *fear*. There can be no *love* when there's *fear*.

See Life's Laws:
3	Thoughts are energy: Loving, or not loving (fear).
4	The energy out, returns in kind.
17	What we hold with energy runs our life.
19	We are quintessentially, beings of energy.
16	We only control ourselves.
21	Real love, once given, cannot be taken back.
22	We consciously only feel our own feelings.
23	Now is the only time there is.

Questions and/or Exercises:
- **Do you** think just maybe, we are talking about marriage—not that there can't be real love in a marriage? But marriage *is* one of society's lies: If you are in love, you get married—right? A few will oblige out of habit, not because they need promises and chains. Society's lie only protects those who are lying about being in love—protection needed, for when the other finds that out. ***Write about it***
- Is it possible that more often than not, marriage acts as a cock-block to real love?
- **The freedom in** real love does not speak to the freedom to "sexually cheat." If there is dishonesty, can there ever be real love*? Write about this too.*

Saying It with Love

There's nothing wrong with you. And there's nothing wrong with me—

It's not even about anyone being wrong. It's just that together—you and me—there's something that just doesn't work.

Our worlds are comprised of how we see life. And our worlds—yours and mine—are just too far apart.

See Life's Laws:
7   Blame is the abdication of responsibility.
13   Our own life is our sole possession. Just so, it is for everyone.

Questions and/or Exercises:
> **The above** is an example of rejecting someone's advances with love. Do you see how it is simply about accepting "what is" without blame? *How could you do it better? If you can think of other loving ways, write about them. This is something you will want to think about now.*

F.U.C.K.

The word is from an mid-fifteenth century English acronym: For Unlawful Carnal Knowledge. But in whose mind was such a God-given natural thing, so piously labeled as carnal—a puritan term of the time meaning sinful? And who was the control freak who made it unlawful? How many minds were damaged by banning such knowledge? Wouldn't it have been so much more nurturing to mankind, had the acronym instead been: For Un-judgmental Connecting Kindness?

Be that so—or not. And some do claim it is not. But then, they're probably just the down-in-the-mouth fans of the rock group Van Halen.

See Life's Laws:
4   The energy out, returns in kind.
3   Thoughts are energy: Loving, or not loving (fear).

Questions and/or Exercises:
- **Do you** see how much of our unconscious beliefs originated from some shit-for-brains asshole from way back when?
- **Are we** now the current irresponsible assholes who unconsciously keep passing those beliefs down to our own children?
- **It's no** longer about anyone's fault—still, don't you think we owe it to them to become more conscious? *Write about it.*

Grit Your Teeth and Buck-up—

The previous reflection, *Saying it With Love,* is about telling you the full truth. Remember the one titled *Omissions*— found in the front of both Books One and Two. You are about to find out why I put something some might see as unimportant, right in your face, first thing.

You see, everything worth having comes with a price. The universe always balances, and *there is a price* to seeing your world differently from most of society. I warned you that change takes courage, and some things in this book would not feel good.

So grit your teeth and buck-up—
These Spiritual Laws —*The Laws of Truth*— will give you a more functional, enjoyable world to live in, but that world remember, is "in here."

What most others see as being *the world,* is still "out there." We all share life, and living yours to the truth of Spiritual Law will still be functional between you and them. Your interactions with others will be peaceful—theirs with you, may not be.

That does not change about those who see the world "out there." You'll find you can see things about them and their lives that they cannot, and that your reactions to life in general will be different from theirs—from what yours once were. Well and good—

Where most go when you don't live your life to suit their own, is drama and control. And they'll demand that you be responsible for their choice of feelings. For most living "out there," it is a simple acknowledgment of their feelings, that is all you need do— *"I'm so sorry you feel that way. . . ."*

It is your relationship with a significant other that will change—y-yup, you've got it—*significantly*. The standard relationship usually involves a lot of control—each demanding the other be responsible for how they, themselves, choose to feel, then arguing and fighting until one accepts that lie, and gives control over to the other.

Then there exists a win/lose relationship, unless both are determined to win, making it a constant lose/lose relationship.

The drama of control isn't love and doesn't leave much room for love—it doesn't leave *any* room, if it's a constant thing. This is what love is like with those who won't take responsibility for their own life and for their own choice of feelings.

If you accept this book, you'll begin seeing life from the view given by these Laws. You become the creator of your life and take responsibility for it, and for your feelings about it all—works for you.

But it will blow your significant other out of the water—they cannot be the winner in that struggle if you are no longer playing the game. Some will see the changes in you and like them. They may even take this same journey. But it is one that you cannot make them take—(Law 13).

This road you're now on has a fork, and for most couples it comes unexpectedly. Each must decide which path they want to take. Life is your personal soul's journey. Yours may well part at this fork—key word "well," because your soul call the shots here. This fork is the omission most teachers of spiritual law leave out.

I do not. This is the price some pay to be the creator of their lives. If you are single—or if your significant has taken that other fork—you may want to keep handy the previous reflection—*Saying it With Love*. It may be useful for a time, before another loving enlightened soul becomes your partner on this journey.

See Life's Laws:
1   I am the creator.
5   For every sorrowful thing, there exists the potential for equal joy. The Universe always balances.
8   The world is not "out there"—it is "in here."
13   Our own life is our sole possession. Just so, it is for everyone.

Questions/exercises to consider:
- **The cost** is great, but the gain is equally so. Would you rather I didn't tell you about *this* cost?
- **Have you** received your invitation from your significant, to play the game of control? It goes something like this: ***"I'm okay, you're all fucked-up."*** Are you still playing?
- **You do** know that in declining, there can be but one answer? ***"I'm so sorry you feel that way."***
- **You do** know how that answer usually results in one action on your part? What is that?
- **To stave** off the pain of it, requires you to do this first: Accept his/her right to be who they are and love them anyway—before you leave. Will you, or have you done that?
- **Do you** understand that there is someone waiting—someone who will understand you, accept you and love you, exactly for who you are? And you cannot meet them until you are beyond your pain?
- **I don't** mean to scare you off—and then, there are those lies of omission I said I wouldn't tell. And I've told you about this price before—it's just that some listen with their head. I'm hoping this time you're listening with your heart. Do you understand that my personal integrity is on the line?
- **Do you** know that I've been here also—and survived? *"I am so sorry this cannot be a feelie-good book. It is the price of your freedom, from the lies."* Write about it all.

PART FOUR

About Politics

and

Spiritual Law

The Collective Consciousness

One needs always be aware that lumping everyone together most often results in disservice. Thing is, with some aspects of life there is a collective consciousness. Such it is in politics

What people do is to look to those who think similarly and to lump themselves into that thinking. That's what politics does. Given there are those who think lovingly and those who don't. Their thinking supports your own—and when your thinking is not loving, you know it. But they then support that unloving part of you. Politics encourages one to be as unloving as one wants, especially when carried to the extremes.

It seems recently, both parties have been gravitating to the extremes. That we have a two party system makes it difficult to be loving and independent. It is the extremes of each party that we consider the unloving parts.

The general ideology of each in recent years is reaching a tipping point. One party now lends itself more of those unloving extremist than the other. This is expressed in its actions.

The truth of one's thinking will ALWAYS be eventually expressed in one's actions.

The following is not so much about Democrats or Republicans, but rather based on their actions. It is about the unequal extremes—and about power. Politics in general, IS, about power.

See Life's Laws:
15—In a functional life one must do one's own thinking.
8—The world is not "out there"—it is "in here."
17—The energy to which we hold fast is what runs our life.
4—The energy out, returns in kind.

Questions and/or Exercises:
- **Is your** thought system one of extremes?
- **Do you** fit into the extreme end of either party?
- **What are** the things you dislike about your party?
- **Are they** Loving or unloving things? *Write.*

Which Side of the Fence

"If you ever wondered what side of the fence you sit on, this is a great test. I wish I could tell you who wrote it, but the copy I had was unsigned. In general, I agree.

If a conservative doesn't like guns, he doesn't buy one.
If a liberal doesn't like guns, he wants all guns outlawed.

If a conservative is a vegetarian, he doesn't eat meat.
If a liberal is a vegetarian, he want all meat products banned for everyone.

If a conservative is down-and-out, he thinks about how to better his situation.
A liberal wonders who is going to take care of him.
If a conservative doesn't like a talk show host, he switches channels.
Liberals demand that those they don't like be shut down.

If a conservative is a non-believer, he doesn't go to church.
A liberal non-believer wants all mention of God and Jesus silenced.

If a conservative decides he needs health care, he goes about shopping for it, or may choose a job that provides it.
A liberal demands that the rest of us pay for his."

Anonymous Author

Left Turn—Right Turn—

Yes, this is not a feelie-good workbook, and there are some who argue that politics breaks with the general theme of this book. It does not. This —Book Two—takes it all a step deeper in asking the questions about which many don't want to get honest. The question of politics is only one, and we haven't even come to "organized" religions, love, and God—yet. This book is about looking at your self—and about honesty. You have what you have—you are who you are. That will never change unless you can see the truth and apply it to yourself with honesty.

And truth?—I suggest you look to the Spiritual Laws, and not the lies of society, politics, or religion. The Spiritual Laws—these Laws of Life—are exactly that: the truth. They are not something this author made-up.

These "in depth" subjects all concern power. Where and how, is power used—or misused?

• There is the power government gives a politician over his/her constituents by virtue of the laws and use of those laws.

There is a like power that religion gives to the preacher by use of the power his/her congregation perceives is wielded by that preacher, supposedly in the name of God.

•In relationships, there is the power one gives to the other concerning the vulnerabilities of the heart.

•In all cases where power is involved, there will be those who will abuse it—teachers, bosses, corporate leaders, spouses, etc.

They use that power to raise someone up, or put someone down—a use determined by whether the wielder lives life in the energy of love or fear. Sadly, where power is concerned, those who are loving, don't need or want power.

And few of those who do want power, will want to look at who they themselves, become while wielding it. This is one reason why this redneck book is so "in your face down and dirty." Nearly everyone alive at some time is involved with the wielding of power. But this book is not asking you to look at others. It is about asking you, to look at you.

——— — — — ———

See Life's Laws:
3   Thoughts are energy: Loving, or not loving (fear)
4   The energy out, returns in kind.

Exercise:
- **Write about** all the places you see power used—is it used lovingly, or un-lovingly.
- **Then take** it home to where—and in what—energy, you use power. Was any of it used lovingly—look again. Some believe that control is necessary. I agree when it is about protecting myself or loved ones from physical harm.
- **Outside of** that, can attempting to control another adult ever be loving.
- **For me,** control over another is never wanted, and seldom needed. *What about you—yeah, write about it?*

Liberals and Conservatives
(a general overview)
And Spiritual Laws

Liberals want to demand that the way they see life—and create theirs—must be the same for you. And they want to use the strong arm of government to make it be so.

Conservatives take responsibility for their own lives—and only their own. They want to use their government's strong arms only for keeping themselves safe from those others who would actually do them physical harm.

Liberals believe that how they see life as being, must be the same way you must see it too. They want to use government to physically control your life—and your mind? They want control of that too—but not their own.

Conservatives don't give a shit about what you think, they only care about what you do. They want no control over you except when you are being injurious to themselves.

With Liberals, whatever the means is okay, because they know what's best for you.

Conservatives only want the freedom to control themselves.

See Life's Laws:
1   I am the creator.
7   Being the creator requires responsibility.
13 Our own life is our sole possession. Just so, it is for everyone.

Questions and/or Exercises:
- Who do you think is the more functional and why?
- When it comes to loving others, which group is the more loving? Why?
- Which group is most apt to be telling themselves lies in order to get what they want? Why?
- Is that because the laws they live by—precepts—of their lives are lies?
- In which group do you think you belong? And why?
- These thoughts are only in general. Some of us refuse to allow those on the far side to push us equally far to either side. We attempt ot see truth and reason. Where do you stand in the cess-pool known as politics?

Repeating History

It has been said:

Those who cannot remember the past are condemned to repeat it.

—George Santayana

History doesn't repeat itself, but it does rhyme.

—Mark Twain

So let's look at Hitler. He built his following upon the ideals of an "Elite Aryan Race." Then he invited all those working class, wanna-be elitists, to bully the rest of the German population into submission. Lastly, he gave them all someone to hate—the Jews.

Sound familiar? Look at our 2016 Presidential race. One side accusing the other of following some "Hitler," while seeing themselves as the "elite." In a shark tank full of political lies, who's to say what is the truth? Near as I can see, only one side has employed wanna-be bully-boys, and yet tried to label the other as being another "Hitler." All the while considering themselves as being the real elite class.

So I have to ask myself: Did America dodge a bullet with the results of this election? Seems so, those "elite" losers now are refusing to accept the will of the people, and are making the winners into their target to hate? What will it take to bring us all back together as Patriotic Americans.

Will it take ISIS becoming that hateful target?—Or North Korea?—Or Iran?

Why is it we are so bent on victimizing ourselves with hate?

Bottom line: *Hate* is the reaction side of *fear*. And *fear* is not *love*. We don't have to lie down and become victims to any of it. Outside of threatening you or your life physically, no one can make you a victim but you. And, what with this socialist nonsense, my way of life—our whole society—is indeed being threatened. So how can I resist being their victim? Resisting through arms, which the 2nd Amendment gives us the ability to do, is one choice—the fearful choice of last resort. No, my choice is to squeal like a hog. When others hear me and start to think for themselves, they too will start squealing and the take-over of our way of life can be stopped.

Squealing may sound like a victim, but the true victims are those whose heads are buried in the sand. I chose to resist all that *fear*, but to resist it in the space of *love*. When others see me loving myself by refusing be a victim, perhaps they too, will choose to join in—and still others will then follow. And it is not even about *me*—It is simply a choice between *love* and *fear*. And I would love to see my government cleaned up by the simple squealing of a hog—one whose head is not buried in the sand, and whose ass is then, no longer presented for the porking.

Taking offense with others, when it is only over our own poor choice of feelings, is senseless. Taking offense with others who threaten us physically, is necessary.

See Life's Laws:
3   Thoughts are energy: Loving, or not loving (fear).
4   The energy out, returns in kind.
8   The world is not "out there"—it is "in here."

Questions and/or Exercises:
- **If you** are a hard-working sweat hog—like I spent my life being—do you believe it your duty to feed those who won't work?
- **Or are** you one of those hogs being fed at the public trough, who keep voting in those dishonest politicians who are buying your vote?
- **Do you** respect yourself enough to work, and love yourself enough not to allow others to run your life?
- **Some bury** their heads in the sand and keep quiet. Who do you know who would unseemly squeal, rather than accept being a victims? *List them. Are you on the list?*

PART FIVE

Reflections of Organized Religion, Spirituality, and a Higher Power

In The Light of The Laws

NOTE:

Most of the examples concerning religion are written as being from the Judeo-Christian standpoint. They are generally valid for other religions, as most are in the "organized" category. Where this book is concerned, it holds that there exists a "higher power."

And about that higher power—the word most used to recognize it, is "GOD." But problems arise, in that we mere mortals have generally been indoctrinated by the use of blinders. Like an old mule pulling the wagon of life, blinders are used to keep that mule focused. And the focus with religions is whatever each chooses to use to define God.

In other words, religions don't want you to think for yourself—or to get distracted, by unauthorized thoughts. Most Christian religions want you to see God as a "being," up there somewhere in a place called Heaven, and apart from you.

For you to be in God's presence requires you to go to one of God's houses, where your connection is somehow dependent on the preacher. Some even require you to be on your knees. Is that out of respect for God, or does it just make it easier to pick your pocket

Enough with the "blasphemous" jokes. For some, this writing will likely rip those blinders right off their virgin minds. When this book says "God" it really means much more than what those blinders ever allowed anyone to see—ah, the bright light of truth, shining into an awakened mind. In writing this book, I was tempted to use the word "SOURCE" in place of "GOD." But it takes time for folks to see beyond what their "organized religions have for so long allowed."Even with blinders the light can be dazzling.

Again:

This is NOT a feely-good book.

The Ocean of God

**I am but a drop
in the Ocean of God.
Not greater than—
Not less than—
Just the same as—
The whole.**

See Life's Laws:
20   We are part of the energy that comprises God.
19   We are quintessentially, beings of energy.

Questions and/or Exercises:
- **Can you** see how we are all in touch with the power?
- Are you aware that we use that power in creating everything in our lives—that we cannot do otherwise?
- **Can you** see how most of our creating is done by the unconscious part of our mind? Please don't give this one an unconscious mono-syllable answer.
- **Doesn't the** fact you are reading this book says you want that creating to be a conscious thing? *Tell me. Or better yet, tell yourself about it. You are the one you need to convince.*

The Truth of Our Being

The truth of our being is that it requires no box, nor does it recognize its limits. The truth requires only the courage to face the unknown of possibility: the greatest of which is the possibility that we are, indeed, one with—and a physical part of—God!

"I am the creator." This is the one Law that those folks steeped in their religion, will choke on. And it is not so much about accepting this Law. This Law just is, regardless of whether you accept it or not. What it is that takes *courage*, is found in the cost—the cost you will pay by the rejection of your friends and relatives, who don't accept it. Yes, this one takes *real courage!*

The lies you may live demand validation from those who are close to you. But when you live the truth, You need make no such demands.
Keep breathing . . .

See Life's Laws:
1   I am the creator.
20   We are part of the energy that comprises God.

Questions and/or Exercises:
- **Do you** think that primitive people are steeped in superstition?
- **How many** of our current great religions began with primitive people?
- **Do you think** that just because we no longer consider ourselves as "primitive," and that our religions are generally termed as "organized," that we are no longer superstitious? ***Write about it.***

Putting the Shame on Sex

In general, our society—and especially our religions—demand that we hide the truth about sex from our children. By making it unacceptable in casual discussion, we hide it—even lie about the healthy nature of it. Is it any wonder the human race experiences sex, with so much dysfunction?

In truth, sex is a gift from our Creator, and a necessity for our very existence. Why does man curse it as wrong—the simple joy of it our religions term as evil—especially when not accompanied by promises and chains? Is it not simply the way God made us to be?

Why don't we treat it as a gift, one to another, and from God? Face it—the perceptions stem from our religions. By what pious insanity, do religious leaders call God out as a liar? Does it not prove that they themselves, and their religions, are the real liars?

——— — — — ———

See Life's Laws:
15   One must do one's own thinking.
20   We are part of the energy that comprises God.
8   The world is not "out there"—it is "in here."

Questions and/or Exercises:
- **Did these** last two reflections blow you out of the water? Am I being too heavy handed?
- **Is it** possible that when dealing with politics and religion, the truth often hurts?
- **Do you** know that this is why most Spiritual Law writers omit, or avoid dealing directly with these issues?
- **Would you** prefer I be like most? *Don't give yes or no answers. We're stepping into the real shit here—write about it.*

Good and Evil?

God, the great Omnipotent, everywhere within everything—

We hear our religions describing God so, and then turning around and limiting God to only the "good," and denying the part described as "evil". Then they would deny us our connection with God, saying God is a being somewhere "out there" in a place apart called "Heaven."

Could it be that they had it right in that first statement? And that we too, are a part of God. And good and evil—the highest and lowest of the energy of it all—it is all there.

It is easy to see "evil" being a part of us. Yet we, being a part of God, makes it a part of God also. To deny any of it cuts us off from the flow, from all of it—from God.

What is the truth of what it means in our lives? We simply have a choice in this, our own part of God, of creation. We get to create it sweet or create it sour—to make our lives a heaven, or a hell—here, within God.

See Life's Laws:
20   We are part of the energy that comprises God.
3   Thoughts are energy: Loving, or not loving (fear).
4   The energy out, returns in kind.
8   The world is not "out there"—it is "in here."

Questions and/or Exercises:
- **Can you** appreciate the sweet, without knowing the sour?
- **Can God** appreciate the good, without knowing the evil?
- **Good—Evil?** Can we know either one, without it being within ourselves?
- **Can God?**—*All simple little questions, but deserving of a lot of ink.*

It Is All Good

One like-minded teaching says: *"It is all good."* I agree. It takes it all to make life: the good and bad—the right and wrong—the sweet and sour—and the love and the fear. We may be duality minded, favoring only the more attractive end of each thing, but life requires it all. If we would but open our minds, we would see the truth in that simple saying:

"It is all good—it is all God."

And the alternative to life—is death. What then, is it like? All "organized religions" claim to know what that looks like, and will freely tell you despite their clear lack of experience. Just as they use your belief in a higher power to control you in life, so to do they threaten you with what will happen after death. Fear and control—that is all the preachers of organized religions have to offer.

Do my own thoughts and beliefs in the truth of these laws, offer more? While not the first to say these things, what I say in this book is offered with love, not fearful control. And I don't regard myself as a preacher. If you do, feel free to tell me to shut-the-fuck-up. I won't—but then I'm just a writer. And you don't have to be my reader. But as long as

you choose to read, I don't have—or want—control over you.

Unlike Organized Religions, I have no interest in holding your spiritual balls hostage, nor in squeezing the life out of them.

See Life's Laws:
10   The purpose of life is for those lessons.
5   For every sorrowful thing, there exists the potential for equal joy. The Universe always balances.
16   We only control ourselves.
1   I am the creator.

Questions and/or Exercises:
- **In that** duality of our thinking, is it possible to appreciate anything in life without knowing its opposite? Can you see the perfection?
- **Do you** see how organized religions have always held us hostage to our belief in a higher power?
- **Is it still** so with you?
- **Of those** who have made their mark on history, how many did so, in defiance of the controlling religion?
- **For your** duality of mind, which is the more attractive: *The Spiritual Laws of Truth vs Organized Religion? They are for the most part, opposites, y'know?*

Free Thinkers

There have always been thinkers—people who observe what happens in the world, correlate action, to reaction, to results. And they listen to what other thinkers say and form their own conclusions. Just so, they listen to their heart and form their own personal connection to God.

Then there are those who just listen to what others say, and accept it as fact. They are not thinkers. Some are just fools—following what their government leaders say is best for them. Some are just religious. For it would seem, that what those who form religions do, is demand all fools to believe as *they say* they themselves believe.

And God . . . Does God fit in there anywhere? Yes. God provides the "authority" that religions depend on, the sword that separates those foolish enough not to do their own thinking, from their personal freedom. Truth is, it is everyone's inalienable right to create their own beliefs, whether it be their connection with God, or how they want their world to be.

The questions to ask are these: Does that government leader do what is best for you? And do those religious leaders really believe what they say? Did God actually appear to one of them and tell them things? Or did someone just see an imaginary sword, to match an imaginary vision of a world, where they themselves wield the power of an all-powerful God—and use it? Then pass it all on, under whatever name they call their religion, in memorial of themselves.

The thinkers are seekers, and will always be free. Those who don't think, give up that freedom to those power mongers who thrive in religions and governments, and who are simply parasites.

And God? Isn't God all-powerful—beyond "want?" God created us all and gives us each the power and freedom to be who we choose to be—free thinker, foolish slave, or parasite. *So choose* . . .

———— — — — ————

See Life's Laws:
8   The world is not "out there"—it is "in here."
1   I am the creator.
2   Thoughts Create.
13   Our own life is our sole possession. Just so, it is for everyone.
15   One must do one's own thinking.
16   We only control ourselves.

Questions and/or Exercises:
> - **Do you** find these thoughts hard to swallow? Why?
> - **Some would** say it is difficult to talk honestly about religion without appearing to bitch-slap it. Is this how you see it?
> - **If so,** would it please you to move on to general spirituality? *Write down how you feel.*

Shepherds and Sheep

This thing called "Religion"—

It is what enables one man, to influence others by the purity and love that lights his heart. It also allows another man to influence the same way, but from the darkness and depravity of a malicious mind.

It will always be so, as long as we are but sheep, willing to be led by the crook of whichever shepherd holds the staff.

Whichever way it is—again—*religion* is but the *civilized* way of saying *superstition*. Both are used by those who would set themselves above it all, in order to control a primitive mind. The question then, must be raised: Is your mind primitive? Or do you think for yourself?

Let's face it folks; religion is really not so much about God, rather it is about shepherds—and sheep.

───── ─ ─ ─ ─────

See Life's Laws:
20   We are part of the energy that comprises God.
15   One must do one's own thinking.
13   Our own life is our sole possession. Just so, it is for everyone.

Questions and/or Exercises:
- **I know** for some, these things I say are often hard to swallow. You do know that there are no such demands being made on you—not by me?
- **All that** I ask is that you pay attention to Law 15 above —*will you?*

The Ego's Expectations

Your ego's expectations of how it must be for you to get what you want, will only guarantee you pain. What your ego wants and what your heart wants, are very seldom the same. For your ego has eyes that can only look outside. It cannot see your heart within.

——— — — — ———

See Life's Laws:
12—Our lives are run first by our needs—then our wants.

Questions and/or Exercises:
> **Do you** think your ego can ever be happy with what you have? *Can you? You are not your ego—there is a difference, y'know?*

Resurrections

As for the resurrection—for me, it has already come. My belief is that the resurrection is indeed about an awakening to a new life, though not of the body. This awakening is of the mind—a change in consciousness. As such, it requires a death—of sorts.

It is a remembering of who we are, and a taking of responsibility. And too, it is the death of blame. It is an ending of looking *out there*, for something or someone on which to place wrongness, in order to own the *rightness*. And it is a beginning of looking *in here*, to the recognition of our own answers. The answers were always here.

See Life's Laws:
8   The world is not "out there"—it is "in here".
7   Blame is the abdication of responsibility.
15   One must do one's own thinking.

Questions and/or Exercises:
- **Do you** believe the "Resurrection" mentioned in the Bible is as a physical thing that most Christian religions say it is?
- **Or do you** think it is a change in consciousness like most "Spiritual" sects seem to think—myself included?

Designated Creator

Who knows what Gods our designated creators be? Still, in this life it is I, who am the creator. Yes! My God created this Earth, and everything in it. Still, of my own life, I get to create it—my way. But my creation is only of my own life, not of someone else's.

See Life's Laws:
1 I am the creator.
13 Our own life is our sole possession. Just so, it is for everyone.
20 We are part of the energy that comprises God.

Questions and/or Exercises:
- ➤ **Do you** get that the great downfall of pretty-much all religions, is that they demand you believe as they do?
- ➤ **Yes, this** book is how I see the Spiritual Laws to be. And no! I have no expectations that you will see it the same. My request is that you take from this book, only what works for you.

Everything We Need

Again: The Universe/God will always provide us with everything we need for our growth. Problem is: we only accept what we think we deserve.

See Life's Laws:
1   I am the creator.
2   Thoughts Create.
8   The world is not "out there"—it is "in here."

Questions and/or Exercises:
- **What has** this book provided you, that you needed for your own personal growth? *Yes—write. . . .*

>>><<<

Soul Experience

It is one thing to learn something and believe it to be true: it is another thing to *know* it to be true. It is just so, with our souls. There is nothing our souls do not know. Yet our soul needs the experience of it—here in this life—to *know*, and to grow.

See Life's Laws:
10   The purpose of life is for those lessons.

Questions and/or Exercises:
- ➢ **Ah, the** great meaning of this life thing—can you believe it is this simple?
- ➢ **What, if** anything, do you think is missing?

In Our Hearts

It is true!
It is not enough to know a thing, up here, in our heads. Our soul is here to experience it; to learn it, as in our hearts. God knows it all. We are the life part, through which God gets to experience life and all life's feelings, as in the emotions of the heart. Just as we are God's taste buds experiencing life, so too, do we experience the emotions of life, the feelings, for God's heart.

It is our job to learn, and in the experience to *know,* for the growth of our soul. And it is our job that through us, God can *know* life's emotional experiences as well. The events and people in our lives are merely there to give us the lessons. The more emotional the feelings, the greater the gift for our soul. And perhaps the greater the experience, for the heart of God.

Yet for us here in this life, none of that matters, if we are unwilling to accept the lessons of the gift offered, and share them. Yes, when we don't accept the lessons, when we would rather blame others for our feelings rather than receive the gift—clearly we cheat our self. Question is, do we also cheat God?

NO! A gift is a gift. And gifts have no strings, no expectations. It is always your choice to win or lose in your life. God does not lose—God does not win—God just experiences!

See Life's Laws:
18   Soul to soul pacts are made in the pre-existence.
10   The purpose of life is for those lessons.
20   We are part of the energy that comprises God.
7   Blame is the abdication of responsibility.

Questions and/or Exercises:
- **What is** God experiencing through you?
- **List the** top 10 or so things that come to mind that God experiences through you?
- *Now own them!*

Enlightenment and the Spiritual Warrior

Enlightenment is what happens when one shines the light of honesty upon ones self. It is to see clearly that we alone, are the creator of our own life, and can no longer blame others for what we create, or how we feel about it.

Nor can we credit some supernatural force or being "out there," for all we might term good or evil about ourselves. Rather, enlightenment is to accept that it is we—ourselves—who are a mixture, incorporating at times either the energy of good, or evil—*loving, or unloving.* To be enlightened is to understand and accept that it is simply an internal choice in every moment of life.

Therefore, to be enlightened, demands we fight an inner battle—become a Spiritual Warrior—those of us who would choose to be loving. For loving is the higher—yet harder to maintain—of the two energies. And too, loving has its own reward: *The Energy Out Returns in Kind*—remember?

See Life's Laws:
8	The world is not "out there"—it is "in here."
4	The energy out, returns in kind.
7	Blame is the abdication of responsibility.
3	Thoughts are energy: Loving, or not loving (fear).
19	We are quintessentially, beings of energy.
15	One must do one's own thinking.

Questions and/or Exercises:
- **Why exactly** did you get this workbook?
- **Were you** consciously wanting enlightenment?
- **If so,** did you know what the term meant?
- **If not,** do you know now? *Explain.*
- Do you have the courage required to be a Spiritual Warrior?

Shining Moments

Some of our most shining moments come, when lighting up the darkness within us—that part we deem so odious, that even we don't want to see, much less smell it. Yet even the foulest of sewer gasses can get ignited. It just takes a spark.

Or maybe for you, it is envisioned that within those dark regions of your mind there lies a powder keg, and that such a spark would blow all semblance of self-respect—indeed, your very life—to hell.

Yet, for those courageous enough to provoke such a spark, it does indeed provide light. Be it an exploding powder keg, sewer gas, or merely lighting the wick of a candle—doesn't matter. Within the light provided we see, and are inspired. There is no bliss more comforting, than to bask in the knowledge of who we really are—to bask in the illumination of our soul.

And that "hell"—that unknown shame we believed was hidden within that fearful darkness? That shame was always our own personal hell, created by a fear-filled mind that did not know—or even consider—having courage.

See Life's Laws:
8   The world is not "out there"—it is "in here."
19   We are quintessentially, beings of energy.

Questions and/or Exercises:
- **Did this** help clear up that previous reflection *(Enlightenment and the Spiritual Warrior)? Explain.*
- **Are you** seeing who you are yet? Have you escaped your personal hell? *Again, tell yourself about it!*

Participation

(Reprinted from Book One)

These reflections are provided for your consideration, written as a personal gift—me to you. But for a gift to really *be* a gift, requires someone to accept it. So let's talk about how this book has been accepted in your life. Has it been welcomed with appreciation for helping you to learn the lessons of your life? Or do you appreciate it, and accept it as part of your search for knowledge—using that search as an excuse to avoid the "doing" part of learning those lessons?

Life *is*, about those lessons, y'know. So let's look at your life, and just how "alive" you are living.

Your willingness to go beyond those questions that only *require* a "yes" or "no," speaks loads about your conscious participation in life. You may want to pay close attention to the questions and/or exercise part of this reflection.

See Life's Laws:
10   The purpose of life is for those lessons.
8   The world is not "out there"—it is "in here."
11   Self-esteem requires integrity.
1   I am the creator.

Questions and/or Exercises:
- **In the** "questions" section, do you have an opinion or experience about a particular reflection that you could express, but won't, preferring to answer with a "yes" or "no"?
- **If your** "yes" or "no" answer was not the truth, do you know you are avoiding the question?
- **If it** was the truth, doesn't that mean you are avoiding the answer?
- **Is your** life one of what is least expected, or is it one of participation?
- **Did you** buy this book for "knowledge," or to help you change your life?
- **Does this** last reflection have your hemorrhoids in a pucker?— You may want to go back through this workbook and do the work you avoided doing.

Religion

Religion is the conscience of the thinking impaired.

It is the *right and wrong* for those who won't think for themselves—and are convinced that *right and wrong* somehow exist outside the judgmental minds of those "holier" than themselves.

See Life's Laws:
3   Thoughts are energy: Loving, or not loving (fear).
15   One must do one's own thinking.

Questions and/or Exercises:
- **Why do** I keep asking you to do your own thinking?
- **Why is** it so important? *Write.*

➤➤➤◄◄◄

Chicken Exits

You may recall how in the Introduction there was the following:
A note here for those who, like myself, are likely to get their sphincter all bound-up over the linguistics of calling these things "Laws." Feel free to call them—"Principles" or "Truisms"—or any other word you choose.

From what I am about to tell you, you may feel that I was setting you up to lose. NOT SO—I was setting you up to see something about you. Something that is true for everyone, but few want to recognize it for what it is: That "something" is our "chicken exits."

Have you ever been to a theme park where they feature that one *really scary ride?* Just before you get on that ride you may have noticed a gate off to the side. That is the "chicken exit". It is for all those who thought they had the courage to do the ride, but at the last moment, *didn't.*

I wanted to give you your chicken exit—but one that would not keep you from taking this ride. Most people don't believe in absolutes. They think that there is always an exception to the rule. If at any point while reading *Book One or Two*, you felt that the law didn't apply, then the truth is, you made yourself the exception to the rule. *You took the chicken exit.*

Again, these laws are like gravity: The only time gravity does not apply—the *apparent* exception—is when we are on a airplane that is in free-fall, or a spacecraft in orbit. "Apparent" because an orbit is simply a free-fall that keeps it falling around the earth. If that spacecraft doesn't make occasional corrections, the orbit will deteriorate. And if the airplane does not re-start its engines—well, the end result in both cases, will be to crash and burn because gravity is still in effect.

If you made yourself the exception to the laws and took any chicken exits, I want you to know that your life doesn't have to crash and burn. Start your engine back up, go back and re-apply these laws to your life as absolutes. Again, like gravity, they are absolutes. The crashing and burning—it is always your free choice to ignore the truth.

--- — — — ---

See Life's Laws:
All of them.

Questions and/or Exercises:
- **Did you** take any chicken exits?—If so, which ones?
- **Have** you gone back and applied the laws as absolutes? *Write about your thoughts on it.*
- **What in** particular, did you have to acknowledge in order ***not*** to take that chicken exit?
- **Do you** regard this as "setting you up to lose"? Or is it a damned good lesson?

Your Conscious Choice

We are all full-spectrum souls. We have it *all* within us—everything from the meanest depths of depravity, to the highest ecstasy of purest love. Were it not so, we could not recognize those things when exhibited by others.

How can a fish truly know the water, until it gets out into the air? Now . . . given this knowledge, from this moment on, *you* are as that fish who has experienced the air. *You,* now know something most others do not. In your journey through these pages, *you* now know the truth about life, about *yours*, and where *you* fit within the spectrum.

The good news is that *you* have free agency in creating *your* life. *You* get to choose just who *you* wish to be—indeed, who *you* are being. And if *you* aren't being everything *you* want—the "who" *you* want to be—*own it!* It is now your conscious choice. *Choose better.*

Yeah, looking at that one, for some, may be painful. If it's not exhilarating for *you*, then make it so. That too, is now *your* conscious choice.

See Life's Laws:
8 The world is not "out there"—it is "in here."
3 Thoughts are energy: Loving, or not loving (fear).
2 Thoughts Create.
25 Every word is an order to our soul.

Exercise:
- **Do you** wonder why I am leaning so hard on the word "you" in this reflection? *Why do you think that is?*
- **Write about** the most important things you have learned from this book. You are summing up your growth here. Don't cheat yourself. Thoughts create, and every word—remember—is an order to your soul.

About Beliefs

If you're not getting what you want, you need to remember that you are getting what you believe you can have. The Universe is built to perform to your beliefs.

See Life's Laws:
2   Thoughts Create.
4   The energy out, returns in kind.

Questions and/or Exercises:
- **What don't** you have, that you want?
- **What is** it about you, that says you can't have it?
- **No—we** are talking about your beliefs—your thinking. *Write about that.*

You Are the Winner!

Among all those countless billions—no, trillions, maybe even quadrillions of souls in this infinite universe—you have won the lottery! You get to live a life on one of the greatest planets in existence—Earth. And more, this life is lived as a member of the most advanced species on the planet. *But hey, you do know that everything worth having comes with a price—remember?*

Now the fact that you are reading, that you even can read, says that you have been enjoying your prize for a time now. Have you recognized the price yet? How so many of those other winners also enjoying their own lives, believe they are entitled—that you owe them a piece of your prize.

For instance it is common for parents to expect you to live your life as they do, to demand you carry-on yours exactly as they would—that you be the next "them." And those folks you rub shoulders with everyday, how most will expect you to live and think the same way they do—even though it causes them no harm if you don't? Oh, and that one special one—that "significant one"— how he or she will likely demand that you allow them to control your life—to force you to live it to suit themselves—so that they will choose to feel good about who you are effortlessly. Yes, pretty fucked-up, wouldn't you say? This whole entitlement thing has always been the norm, but these days it has been re-labeled, "progressive thinking"—even though it leaves no room for the progress of a person's soul.

And then there is your religion. It especially, expects you to live this sacred prize—your life—the way they demand. Maybe that is because they would wield the power of the Universe—the power of God—*if, you would let them.* They would convince you that everything good you get is a gift from God—but only if you bow to their evangelical line of bullshit. Of course all the bad stuff—that comes from those other mundane souls around you, or from your government, or even just this world. If you step too far out of their clutches, they threaten you with some mystical beast they call "The Devil" who will torture you with fire—a bit superstitious don't you think?

Of them all, they want you to be held captive to their wishes—a slave. They all demand you give your life to them. They want you to believe you are a victim—same as them.

But you—you have won the lottery, once more. You have discovered the truth. Among them all, you are one of the rare conscious ones. But with nearly every one you know—even those close who have sworn their love to you—you will find the price for you to think differently, is often found in their inability to then accept you.

You've read this book. And while it doesn't tell you much that you mightn't have read in other books, perhaps this

one you read with your heart, and not just your mind. Perhaps in seeing the price you pay—probably are already paying—you can see the great value in these truths.

Painful? Yes, but pain is one of those indicators the Higher Power of the Universe has given us to point out the way. Here on Earth, you don't *win*, rather you *earn* that next great lottery. You are one of the few who has learned the lessons, seen the lies, and experienced the truth of life—and evolved your soul through that experience. You might not see it, or believe this yet, but you will. *And you will find that the price was worth it!*

——— — — — ———

See Life's Laws:
This reflection encompasses every one of the laws as given.

Questions and/or Exercises:
- **The price** is high—I paid it too. Most authors writing about Spiritual Laws omit telling you the full truth. Are you glad I did? *Write about it.*
- **Much of** what this book tells you—including this—is repeated in different scenarios. Did this work for you. Or is this the first time you truly heard it—in your heart and not just your head? *Again, write about it.*
- **Y'know, a** lot of folks don't get the point until the scenario matches up with their lives. Did you get that match-up earlier? *Yup. Write, tell yourself about it.*

Now On to the Next Lottery

Are you feeling pretty special for having won these last two lotteries? Are you ready to win the next one—the one where you will evolve beyond it all? You are here on Earth, and you have realized your connection to the power of all the Universe—that you are in actuality, a part of God. And you have taken responsibility for your life and everything in it. Undoubtedly you have even begun to share your love in the service of those who need you. What more can there be to evolve into without dying? It is a simple thing really—*it is to touch the love of that God-part within you.*

What?—What the fuck does that mean?

It is not something you learn, not something you do, not even something for you to "be." It is something you *feel* with all the passion of your being —GRATITUDE!

Gratitude for all you have become.

Gratitude for all who have played their respective parts for you—or you for them—in life.

Most of all, gratitude for the beauty in all the Higher Power's creations in your life.

> *The wind through your hair.*
> *The never-to-be-repeated shapes in the clouds above.*
> *The raindrops on your face.*
> *And afterwards, the clean smell of ozone in the air.*
> *The buzz of a honey bee, adding to your life its own special sweetness.*
> *The flight of a humming bird.*
> *The colors of its plumage, and of the flowers from which it sips.*
> *Or of the rainbow in the distant sky.*
> *Then there is the gold of a sunset—and the joy that comes with the next sunrise.*

Whatever price you have—or will—pay for changing your mind, considerate it worth it: PAID, done deal. EVERYTHING in this world—and every experience you have, you now get to meet with GRATITUDE.

Your life means nothing without it!

———— — — — ————

See Life's Laws:
Again, this one needs no laws listed in explanation—and no questions asked—it just needs one exercise. You know what that one is . . .

The Choice

In all the Universe, in the whole infinite vastness of it all, what is there if there is not life? And Life?—What is life, if there is not sentience—self-aware, feeling, thinking, creative intelligence?

Some believe the Universe—the all-encompassing whole of it all—is God, the omnipotent, all powerful, within everything, everywhere. *That God!* And everywhere in the Universe that life can develop, it does. Does it not appear, that throughout it all—that God—is geared toward bringing forth life. And life? Again, what is the pinnacle of life, if it is not sentience? Would that not describe us?

And if we are of such importance—or perhaps pleasure—for God, then wouldn't God want to nurture us? Would God give us the ability to hope and dream and conceive? And, wouldn't that say that God serves us? So why do religions say that we are only here to serve God? Does God—the omnipotent all-powerful everything—really need someone, who those religions would place outside of God's all-encompassing self, to be a servant? Or do we merely serve as one, inside, together?

Consider: We are all part of the energy of the Universe—part of God—aren't we? Assuming that the energy of the Universe IS God—and being a part of God called sentient life, how do we fit into it all? Could it be that we are the taste buds by which God gets to feel/taste/experience life? For what is sentient life, if not thinking, feeling, experiencing beings? And can one know the sweet, without tasting the sour? Can one ever feel the loving if there is not some opposite fearful *other* thing?

And doesn't cultivating this buffet require we have free choice in our feelings, and in our being?

Yes WE, being a part of this all-encompassing wholeness many, including I, believe is "God,"—WE, being the highest, sentient pinnacle of the life part of creation—WE get to choose to be the best, or the worst of God's life experiences. WE get to be the sweet or the sour.

So . . . make your choice! *Do you want to be the loving, or not loving experience of God.*

See Life's Laws:
- 3   Thoughts are energy: Loving, or not loving (fear).
- 5   For every sorrowful thing, there exists the potential for equal joy. The Universe always balances.
- 20 We are part of the energy that comprises God.
- 24 What we dwell upon with energy—is what we attract.
- 4   The energy out, returns in kind.

Questions and/or Exercises:
- ➢ **How much** of your life do you spend in the energy of love, as opposed to fear?
- ➢ **Knowing that** you are as a taste-bud by which God tastes life, will that ratio now be changing?
- ➢ *List everything about yourself that is sweet.*

Taste-buds of God

What's it all mean? Here at the end, let me leave you with a few personal thoughts—some crudely esoteric redneck shit—shit that you may think, stinks.

In Book One there is a reflection entitled "Fear." It was explained that there is a duality that we insist on defining everything as being between. And in the center, there is a tipping point—as in between sweet and sour there is tasteless. Between love and fear there is indifference. Is it possible the God resides at that tipping point—or maybe in the center of an infinitely large circle of life? Clearly at a place that is beyond our understanding—mine, yours, everyone's. . . .

Is God simply an infinite indifference—a point of tastelessness—a neediness? Is that why God is so bent on creating life: Life that can and does fill that space with our choice of energy—love or fear? Are we indeed, the taste-buds of God, experiencing life? Or more—maybe we are God's entertainment system?

God is the great enigma. How or what God is? It's all speculation—us, trying to make sense of the indefinable—something beyond our ability to understand.

Here's a real redneck speculation: What if God were like a big cat licking its fur. Would Mankind be as a fur-ball in that cat's shit—shit that has nourished the cat. Now that statement will make a few folks cough in indignation. Still, what if. . . .

Point is: if anyone tells you they KNOW what God is, just picture a big turd of hairy cat shit they've painted pink—because that is what that person has between their ears. NO one knows what God is.

Irreverent? Me—irreverent? Certainly not where God is concerned. Although I believe God would be way beyond any need for our reverent worshipful adulation. To me, God just is. Does He/She/It care about what we think? Personally, I think God only cares that we feel and experience life. Where we are concerned, maybe God has a cat-shit sense of humor.

Accchhhh—errraacccchhhh—aaaaachhhhttt.

Excuse me while I hack up this hair-ball. Wouldn't want it to become immersed in all that shit between my own ears. That's right! Haven't I too, been telling you who God is?

I too, simply don't know. I believe you've got to die to truly know. What I do know is that I have been to the edge of that cliff and have caught a glimpse—but only a small one. One just large enough to help me see through all this "religion" crap and to know a little of the truth.

The truth?—It can be anal-ogized to WD 40. That's right—the penetrating oil. It can seep down through even the smallest crack. Like truth, if the vessel has any holes in it, WD 40 will leak through. These rules—these Laws—are the vessels I've found that will hold truth.

Is God—as many believe—composed of the energy of all the universe? Or is God something else, maybe the space between and all around all those particles of that energy, an eternal nothingness that is everything.

The enigma . . .the unfathomable . . . the indefinable . . . the. . . .

Hell, does it really matter? For us mortals, what matters is the truth. The lies we have all been taught to believe, just . . . DON'T . . . FUCKING . . . WORK. The truth does.

I told you in the beginning that I wouldn't lie—nor tell you half-truths. I bet you didn't expect all this here at the end. Sounds almost like a disclaimer.

So now, let me take this on out there into the outfield, with some of my own personal beliefs. Thing is, these Spiritual Laws, they've been around probably since the dawn of religion and before. Ever since our kind began to understand that there must be some higher power—some intelligence much greater than us.

These Spiritual Laws of Truth operate on the principal that we are a part of—in fact, a piece of that higher power. And that we actually wield that power in the very creation of our own lives. You may have seen the movie or read the book, *The Secret*. If you did, you probably recognized it in the laws presented here in this book—only expressed differently.

Law One—I am the creator.

It is exactly—and literally so. We do create our lives, and we do it with our thoughts.

And religions?—So long as we can make the connection with that Higher Power—with God—in our minds, does it really matter. It is not for me to say that your religion is false, that it is wrong. But what I think as being dysfunctional, is the greed and lust for power in some of the men—or women—who would use your beliefs in that religion for personal gain or glory.

Yes, given that we actually wield the power of creation—though in this mortal life we wield it slowly. What about when we leave this mortal body and are spirit—*a Soul on that God level?* Wouldn't it be logical that we will wield it instantly?

And of God, *the Great Essence of the Infinite*—can you see that while we know in our heads about infinity, we do NOT know it in our hearts? Has anyone alive ever experienced it? Infinity is beyond the grasp—the understanding—of us mere mortals. So why can't all religions be true, at least in their beliefs concerning the after-life? Isn't it safe to say that pretty-much all religions are concerned with, and have at least some, beliefs about an after-life?

In that after-life, why can't Catholics have their Catholic heaven—even their hell? Mormons don't believe in hell, but why would that stop them from having their three degrees of glory—all of it exactly as they believe? And can it not also be so for all other religious beliefs?

Even Islam—as I understand it the Koran doesn't specify, but some Muslim men are being promised seventy-two virgin wives. Not to insult their Heaven—all I can say is that they must be more man than I. That many wives would wear me down to a stub in no time. Gotta wonder what I'd do with the rest of eternity

Me? I know that eventually I will be punching out on the great time-clock of life. And I believe in reincarnation—so like Arnold says, ". . . I'll be back." But unlike many others who also hold this belief, it won't be as a bug.

And God?—Perhaps my God is only limited to the ability of my personal perceptions. This book is only meant to open your mind to the infinite possibilities—not to limit it by my own. My own personal truth about God is my own—yours is yours. *It doesn't . . . fucking . . . matter . . . if they don't match.*

So long as it doesn't, then that makes us—you and me—organized religion's greatest nightmare. Religions are in the business of separating us from God, and then selling God back a little piece at a time.

And religions require that everyone have ONLY one truth concerning a Creator. They still—to this day—are killing one another over something so esoterically fucked-up.

Governments want control of your life—religions want control of your mind. Both want to steal your money.

I vote for who I want in government—ignore organized religion—and the money? Hell, we all pay a fair share to run the hog farm.

For the most part, my life is peaceful and happy. I run it on love, and—to the best of my ability—observe the Spiritual Laws.

If you can grasp that, perhaps God has taught you something about experiencing infinity—or maybe just in making your own choices on how you choose to think and feel. But hey . . . it's just a thought. And we know about thoughts now, don't we?

See Life's Laws:
This is pure personal speculation—based on all the Laws as this redneck understands them. Why else title this book **Redneck Spirituality?**

Questions/exercises to consider:
- **Write down** *your own thoughts and speculations. Unless you want to write your own book, limit it to 10—or maybe—15,000 words.*
- **If you've** used this space to take offense—this far in—ya gotta know that I've failed you as a companion on your journey. **Write about that.**
   If you did, there is a concept in this book titled "taking offence." Re-read it. Did you agree, or did you double-down? Write about that.

One and The Same

When you want to hurt someone—when you want revenge—ask yourself; is this what I would want to do, if he were me? For he is you, y'know? —And I am too. You're hurting all of us. Like love, hurt is a feeling we give to ourselves. It too, has nothing to do with others. Yet it too, is felt by all. On that level beyond consciousness, we are all one and the same—you and I—and all of humanity.

And too—Aren't we also a part of God?

See Life's Laws:

20   We are part of the energy that comprises God.
1   I am the creator.
4   The energy out, returns in kind.
19   We are quintessentially, beings of energy.

Questions and/or Exercises:
- **What do** you believe God—that Higher Power—is?
- **There is** order—structure—laws that govern the workings of the Universe. God perhaps? *What do you think?*
- **Are we** all not part of the energy of the Universe? *Any thoughts on that?*

Epilogue

Both books in this series are an in-your-face redneck experience. I wrote them that way on purpose. Most folks will never get honest about their lives until the shit's in their face. Even then, they don't like to acknowledge the truth of it. That truth is just as this title suggests. Shit points out what stinks in life. So, take it on home—in YOUR LIFE.

You've got that correctly—this book is about your life, about looking at it and learning those lessons—the ones right now in your face. And yes! They're gonna stink.

Again, shit is what's nourished you. Doesn't matter if that shit is coming out of your butt, or leaking from between your ears. Difference is, when coming from one end, it just needs to be flushed. But when from the other—yeah, it's gonna stink, and its gonna be in your face. To flush it, you're gonna need to change something in your thinking. And that, is gonna change your whole life. And too, what your life then becomes, doesn't stink.

Skid stains in your face or in your shorts—do you really want to meet the Angel of Death with either end stinking? Going to your grave is a sure-thing. The stinking is not.

What Then

When I die . . . when I'm dead . . . what then?
Who will be there to watch the ashes fall?
Into space . . . into eternity . . .
To mix and become one with the good red soil,
in the cool shady canyons
beneath those magnificent,
sheer sandstone cliffs . . .
the ancient homeland,
of the Anasazi.

Perhaps I was one, in a former life.
I feel a kinship there, a homecoming.
And what of this life?
Will there be a hole
in the fabric of humanity?
Whose lives have I touched?
Is this world a better place
because I drew breath?
Will there be multitudes
to shed bitter tears,

Or will it be a mere blink,
a single tick of the clock of humanity,
before all remembrance
and trace of me will vanish.
Except for a fragment of bone,
lodged under a rock
in some dry watercourse . . .

Or a few molecules of magnesium
nurturing a cedar . . .
Potassium in a flower . . .
Or perhaps, some calcium in the
tooth of a playful little chipmunk.
I will become a part of, and one,
with the canyon lands.
It is enough. . . .

And sometime perhaps,
my soul will reincarnate.
And I will once again
walk these desert plateaus . . .
drink from the cool springs,
deep in the shadowy canyons.
And perhaps,
I will sit in the shade of a cedar . . .
Admire the perfection of a wild flower . . .
Even laugh at the antics
of a joyful little chipmunk.
And perhaps, I already have. . . .

The question for you is not "WHAT THEN," it is WHAT NOW? You wouldn't be reading this book if you were not becoming aware of the lies we have all been taught upon which we "should" base our lives. You are searching for truth—and you have found some.

You are now forever changed.
You now know truths
you cannot deny.

Oh you may slip and slide around a little, but you will always come back to these truths. And you will find yourselves living them. Your life will become much more peaceful and functional—although many of the people who were once there, will be gone. And some will be missed.

Those who replace them will also be loved.
For you now know better how to love.
And when "WHAT THEN" eventually comes,
you will rejoice in the life you have lived

FROM NOW.

About The Assessment

At this point you might consider whether you have read—and done the exercises in—Book One. If you have not, I highly recommend that you do so **now**. If you will do that, then do **NOT** turn this page and finish this assessment now. For if you do,

YOU WILL BE CHEATING YOURSELF.

REDNECK SPIRITUALITY

Book One

Don't Paint Your Turds Pink

by

E. Egorhh Frank

The Assessment

Go back through your workbook/s and reassess those reflections upon which you placed a circle of resistance. If you find you no longer feel that resistance, then checkmark it—and it is okay if you still have resistance.

For those who have chosen not to do Book One, the following is necessary information from that book: These workbooks are not about being *right* or *wrong*. I hope you can see and understand that by this point. This book is *only* about seeing the workings of *The Laws of Truth* in your life. It does not have to be the same for *you* as it is for me. The point of this book is to give you some real truth —*the Laws*— and then to get you to look within yourselves.

This assessment is to tell you if it did that, and if there has been any change in your thinking. If there has, then this book has been instrumental in changing your life—*change your mind, change your life.* Remember?

In the beginning, you were asked to get a notebook, preferably one that is a binder, to do the questions and exercises. You were asked to write only on the right side pages. Here is one further exercise for you. Consider doing this one with a different colored ink pen.

Exercise:
> Go over the original questions and answers. If there are any you would now answer differently, put a line through those parts you would change, and use the blank left side sheets to write in your changes. Having since gone through this book and hashed out the meanings of how the laws apply, any changes you make here is an indication of how you have evolved—and know, this doesn't mean your original answer was wrong. There is no right or wrong, remember. There is only truth and love—or not love. What this assessment indicates, is how much better you now see truth, and how much more capacity you now have to love.

Now for the most important part of this exercise
At the beginning of this assessment you were asked to check off on those circles of resistance. Take special note of any reflections you might have marked with a an exclamation point. Have you checked them off, or do you still feel resentment? If you do, then that's okay.

Just understand: There is no attack intended with anything I have written here—and even if you think you see an attack, you have to admit that it cannot possibly be an actual physical thing.

Correct?

A physical attack must be met with resistance. Any other attack is only one of perception—*your own perception*—regardless of what you think was the other person's intent. Perceiving it as an attack, is how people who see themselves as victims, assure they will be. If you are still taking offense, then the working part of both books *now must ask its most important question:*

Questions—Just one to consider:
> *How much longer do you intend to see yourself as a victim in life?*

You see, the basic premise of these spiritual laws is the truth—that being, it is a choice. We have all been taught to be victims in life.

AND THE TRUTH IS: WE ARE NOT!
WE ARE THE CREATORS.

Do you not yet understand what that means? It means that we are WHO we want to be, and we HAVE what we want to have in life. If it is not what we think we want then, we must seek out the truth of why it serves us.

BECAUSE IT DOES SERVE US!

You will almost always see that if it goes against Spiritual Law, it is because we are choosing to see ourselves as that victim we were taught to be.

IT IS A CHOICE:
TO BE THE VICTIM, OR THE CREATOR.

The service being a victim gets you, is that you don't have to be responsible for anything—and you get to suck up the sympathy of others,

LIKE A PSYCHIC VAMPIRE.

Look at the following truth about resentment:

ONLY VICTIMS RESENT!
ONLY VICTIMS TAKE OFFENSE.
ONLY VICTIMS, GO CRYING TO OTHERS—
SUCKING THEIR ENERGY FOR VALIDATION.

When you get fully disgusted with being a psychic vampire—blaming others, and believing yourself a victim—

YOU WILL CHANGE.
And you will then become a true

CREATOR.

About The Author

—Publishers prefer this section to be written in third person, even though it is generally written by the author. No lies, remember?

These days how much of what politicians say can you take as "truth?" It is the same with those in academia. Most are just "talking heads" when it comes to what's true in life. Unless or until, they have learned the truth in their real life—they don't . . . fucking . . . "know."

Speaking of real life, most folks, myself included, don't . . . fucking . . . look—until they are faced with the reality of their own death. You won't find any letters of accolade behind my name, except for the one on this book's title page—and that one, only because it is the name by which some have known me.

About now, you might be saying to yourself "Oh my God, what's this about the 'F' bomb?" Yes, I'm a redneck and we often toss that bomb around like a football. We do it because we know that wherever it lands will become the focus of the whole damn game.

The story of my life can be found in the back of Book One. But Book Two is more advanced—that being said, here is the "rest-of-the-story."

Twenty-five years ago, while lying in a hospital bed, knowing the imminent presence of death, I realized my life had been no more than skid-marks in the shorts of the life I *wished* I'd lived. I swore an oath to that "presence" that whatever life might remain, would be used in searching out life's great truths, and becoming someone such as would fill those shorts without stain or stink—a tall order for someone who had no clue how.

I was only just beginning, to see my life's lies. So I started hanging out with others also searching for truth: New Age, New Thought groups, meditating and reading books about truth—about Spiritual Law.

Then, for several years I worked on the support teams for one of the two personal growth—experiential—seminars companies with which I had experience. By then, my life was based on these Spiritual Laws, and had become peaceful, and functional.

Wanting to pass that on to others, I took accredited coach training from Coach University, and upon graduating, opened a practice as a Personal Life Coach.

Coaching clients in finding the joy missing from their lives was immensely satisfying during those years—the head-hunting part required to make it lucrative, was not. Then for the next twelve years I drove Para Transit buses, taking people with various disabilities where they needed to go. Most desperately needed the help, and for me, being of service to them, was also gratifying.

I seldom coach one-on-one these days. Mostly now, it is with these written words. Still, Coaches need a clear contract, an admission by the client that they want the coaching—and preferably are willing to pay for it. I take it on faith that I have that contract with you—hopefully you bought this book—and after all, you are still spending time reading it.

None of this negates the fact that I am a redneck. And rednecks generally love motorcycles—a fifty year love affair for me. This fact weighs heavily on the reason for this writing.

Riding alone is enjoyable, and riding with others having like-minded joys is even more so. As such, I was one of the original five who started up the American Legion Riders in Nevada. Through my connections in the ALR—I later became the first Nevada State Captain for the Patriot Guard.

Originally started by ALR riders in Kansas, for the purpose of non-violently protecting funerals from religious zealots, and to honor our nation's heroes who have paid that ultimate price of freedom, the Guard was a fine, even cathartic, experience for me.

But for me it was—at least in part—a pressing need. My own service during the Vietnam "conflict" was as a sole survivor. Since just after WW II—1948—the armed services have had a policy that when notified that a soldier is the last surviving male member in a family, the parents can apply for that status and their son will not be stationed in a war zone. I did not know until years later that mine had.

There are 58,267 casualties listed on the Vietnam Memorial Wall—and that does not count the suicides, agent orange, and war wound deaths that occurred later. Reflecting on how I floated past Vietnam on a free pass always came with a sense of shame. Honoring those making the ultimate sacrifice in this current war, for me, became a very personal thing. It was akin to honoring that GI back then, who might have died in my place.

Most of the thoughts in this book were written years ago, and considered private. There was little inclination felt to share them—

until my experiences in the Patriot Guard. It shook me to the core to stand in flag lines with a hundred other teary-eyed patriots, mostly rough tattooed veteran bikers, like myself—to honor yet another fallen hero. And then to realize: It is the consciousness of this world, which makes such sacrifice necessary.

> ***And I knew about consciousness—***
> ***knowledge I'd written so much about, but wasn't***
> ***sharing in any appreciable way.***

The Patriot Guard was a healing experience in my life, but nothing comes without a price. After meeting the presence of the Angel of Death, I learned those laws of truth, and began living my life accordingly. But life balances—being no longer acceptable by my loved ones was the price I paid for seeing life differently.

Those who are closest to you are usually there because your thinking validates their own. I was no longer pretending to be that "good Mormon son"—or the limp-dick controllable husband.

All I've ever had on this earth is my life, and not enough time to live it. But living it my way—with love and joy—was not acceptable to those who wanted my life lived their way. Even so, that price was paid long before the Patriot Guard. And that price was worth it.

In the Patriot Guard—besides tears—the price of my healing included physical pain and discomfort. There were icy winter winds numbing my cheeks, freezing my fingers and chilling my shaking body as I rode north in twenty-three degree weather to honor another hero killed in action. My misery seemed equal to that of the silent yucca trees parading past, their tortured arms up in frozen salute.

And later, with a blistering summer sun liquefying the tar in the pavement beneath my wheels, I carried my nation's flag for many more final salutes—other heroes KIA. Here too was pain as the twin pipes of my exhaust baked this veteran's chestnuts, and the rush of scorching air coming off that highway stung my finger tips, while the burning steel of the grips blistered the palms of my hands.

And then there was the sweat that trickled down my butt crack, moistening—but not staining—my shorts.

*But none of this was more uncomfortable than
the shame of not doing all I knew I could.*

For me, there is joy in holding my life in the twist of my grip on the throttle. Knowing I am the absolute creator, in riding my own life's highway, and feeling the thundering rumbling power with the clench of my butt cheeks in the saddle. But now I can no longer shirk my responsibility. It is now time to just fart and get on with it, and to share this—my own simple attempt to raise the consciousness of anyone riding behind. Perhaps you might be inclined to view that fart, imparted between the pages of this book in all its glorious crudity, as the sad bottom-line of my life.

Not me—this is not the skid-marks of my bottom line, rather this ink represents the highest and best I've ever been.

And crudity? If this redneck is anything like the rest, crudity is simply a coping mechanism for dealing with those heart wrenching moments. Perhaps you can decide on the truth of that matter for yourself—and forgive me for the crudity of my humanity.

Or maybe, forgive yourselves—those of you inclined to make my humanity somehow . . . wrong?

Despite all that inspired me in writing this book, it is not about me, or my redneck crudity—not even about skid-marks. It is about you. YOU: another soul who wants to love, and be loved—*without the pink paint*. It is about you too, being the best you can be, showing-up in the naked honesty of who you are right here—

RIGHT NOW.